The Promise of a
Mother's Prayers

Scharlotte Rich

The Promise of a
Mother's Prayers

Claiming God's Extravagant Love for Your Family

NAV**P**RESS®

BRINGING TRUTH TO LIFE

OUR GUARANTEE TO YOU

We believe so strongly in the message of our books that we are making this quality guarantee to you. If for any reason you are disappointed with the content of this book, return the title page to us with your name and address and we will refund to you the list price of the book. To help us serve you better, please briefly describe why you were disappointed. Mail your refund request to: NavPress, P.O. Box 35002, Colorado Springs, CO 80935.

The Navigators is an international Christian organization. Our mission is to reach, disciple, and equip people to know Christ and to make Him known through successive generations. We envision multitudes of diverse people in the United States and every other nation who have a passionate love for Christ, live a lifestyle of sharing Christ's love, and multiply spiritual laborers among those without Christ.

NavPress is the publishing ministry of The Navigators. NavPress publications help believers learn biblical truth and apply what they learn to their lives and ministries. Our mission is to stimulate spiritual formation among our readers.

ISBN 1-57683-684-3

Cover design by studiogearbox.com
Cover photographs by Jutta Klee/CORBIS
Creative Team: Terry Behimer, Laura Barker, Kathy Mosier, Arvid Wallen, Angie Messinger

Some of the anecdotal illustrations in this book are true to life and are included with the permission of the persons involved. All other illustrations are composites of real situations, and any resemblance to people living or dead is coincidental.

Unless otherwise identified, all Scripture quotations in this publication are taken from the HOLY BIBLE: NEW INTERNATIONAL VERSION® (NIV®). Copyright © 1973, 1978, 1984 by International Bible Society. Used by permission of Zondervan Publishing House. All rights reserved. Other versions used include: the *New American Standard Bible* (NASB), © The Lockman Foundation 1960, 1962, 1963, 1968, 1971, 1972, 1973, 1975, 1977, 1995; the *New King James Version* (NKJV). Copyright © 1982 by Thomas Nelson, Inc. Used by permission. All rights reserved; the *Holy Bible*, New Living Translation (NLT), copyright © 1996. Used by permission of Tyndale House Publishers, Inc., Wheaton, Illinois 60189. All rights reserved; and the *King James Version* (KJV).

Library of Congress Cataloging-in-Publication Data
Rich, Scharlotte.
  The promise of a mother's prayers : claiming God's extravagant love
for your family / Scharlotte Rich.
    p. cm.
  Includes bibliographical references.
  ISBN 1-57683-684-3
  1. Mothers--Religious life. 2. Motherhood--Religious aspects--Christianity.   I. Title.
BV4529.18.R55 2006
248.8'431—dc22

                                        2005036210

Printed in the United States of America

2 3 4 5 6 / 10 09 08 07 06

FOR A FREE CATALOG OF NAVPRESS BOOKS & BIBLE STUDIES,
CALL 1-800-366-7788 (USA) OR 1-800-839-4769 (CANADA)

Children are a gift from the LORD;
    they are a reward from him.
—PSALM 127:3, NLT

Love is patient, love is kind. It does not envy, it does not boast, it is not proud. It is not rude, it is not self-seeking, it is not easily angered, it keeps no record of wrongs. Love does not delight in evil but rejoices with the truth. It always protects, always trusts, always hopes, always perseveres.

    Love never fails.
—1 CORINTHIANS 13:4-8

Contents

Acknowledgments

To my mother for her love and example. To my NavPress friends for their dedication and hard work. To my editor, Laura Barker, a godly mom, for her professional excellence and ideas. To my daughters for their godly examples as good moms and for all the joy they give. To my prayer sisters for their prayers, encouragement, and wonderful advice. To my husband, Dan, a godly father and faithful partner in prayer.

Where's My Instruction Manual?

Does anyone have the foggiest idea what sort of power we so blithely invoke? Or, as I suspect, does no one believe a word of it? The churches are children playing on the floor with their chemistry sets, mixing up a batch of TNT to kill a Sunday morning. It is madness to wear ladies straw hats and velvet hats to church; we should all be wearing crash helmets. Ushers should issue life preservers and signal flares; they should lash us to our pews.
—Annie Dillard on prayer and God's power in *Teaching a Stone to Talk*

Mother's love may sometimes fail. But God's love can use even the imperfect love of an imperfect mother to shape his perfect design in the life of her child.
—Elisa Morgan, MOPS International

As moms we often feel overwhelmed and inadequate. Computers, cars, and other complicated things come with instruction manuals, but children don't. How did mothers in the past—with no modern conveniences, advice books, pediatricians, children's dentists, dinosaur macaroni, or talking books—raise happy, healthy, and godly children?

They began by praying and using the Bible as their guidebook—and so can we.

The Bible has been called God's love letter to the world. Love is the defining characteristic of our heavenly Father's every touch on our lives, and we can have no better guide to mothering than the example of our divine Parent. When love is the basic foundation for raising our children, a lot of the idealistic pressure we put on ourselves dissolves.

Using 1 Corinthians 13—"the love chapter"—as a guide, *The Promise of a Mother's Prayers* gives hope and a smile to tired moms. You can use it as a daily or weekly devotional—or simply open up to whatever chapter speaks to the day's concerns. You may even want to use this book as the basis for a moms' support and prayer group.

However you decide to use it, you'll find lots of real-life stories, biblical insights, and down-to-earth encouragement. With each reading, you'll be reassured that God walks by your side and that you're exactly the mother he knows your children need. Together we'll explore how we can become effective intercessors for our families, claiming God's promises for our kids. We'll also look at some easy and fun positive parenting plans for the future. Most important, *The Promise of a Mother's Prayers* takes seriously the highs and lows of motherhood, offering some hard-earned advice and uplifting affirmation from moms who have been there.

Motherhood changes us, and that's a good thing. For many of us it's the first relationship we have that's mostly give and little take. These precious lives are our mission fields, entrusted to our care by God. Moms are on holy ground. Yet being a mother rarely feels holy, does it? Our holy ground sometimes feels like a battlefield instead.

My children are grown, but sometimes I still think about the times I blew it as a mother. The great thing is that my kids don't remember many of those mistakes that seemed so big to me. They do, however, remember the good things. They remember that I loved and cherished them. I chalk that up to God's patient love and amazing grace. I claimed a lot of God's promises for them from the first day I knew I was pregnant. And God keeps his promises.

God uses the lessons of motherhood to mature us while we help our children grow. As a Christian mom, I have a lot in common with the disciple Peter. Imperfect Peter kept stumbling, but he never quit. Through it all, Jesus loved him and helped him grow into a mountain of a man for God. Peter's life demonstrates that God's promises are for imperfect people. That gives me hope, because I'm not perfect.

My prayer for you is that you will enjoy your children and pour God's love into raising them. They won't be young forever. When their crazy antics get you down, envision their future. Strip away everything else and ask yourself, *Today, what are the most important things I need to teach, say to, and do with my kids?* Maybe it's just to play with them. Treasure the exciting promise and possibility that God has placed in your children. One day they'll be adults whom you have helped fashion. Ask God to give you a vision for what he wants them to become.

As mothers, we touch the future and affect eternity itself with the things we build into our children's lives. That's a huge responsibility and privilege. But we don't walk alone; we walk with the guidance and love of a mighty God and his promises.

God's Promises

My children and I will not want for anything God sees we need, including wisdom.

> The LORD is my shepherd;
> I shall not want. (Psalm 23:1, NKJV)

> "If you then, being evil, know how to give good gifts to
> your children, how much more will your Father who is in
> heaven give good things to those who ask Him!" (Matthew
> 7:11, NKJV)

"Call to Me, and I will answer you, and show you great and mighty things, which you do not know." (Jeremiah 33:3, NKJV)

A Mother's Prayer

Thank you, Lord, for each of my children. Please walk with me and show me what I need to know as I raise them and depend on your promises. Show me the vision you have for their lives. Thank you for always being there when I call to you.

Thank you for being a strong and loving Shepherd to my children. Please protect them from evil and help them grow to love you and your Word. Thank you for the good gifts you have for them.

Positive Parenting Plans

- List a few of your priorities as a mother. Include the things you most want to teach your children and the things you want God to do in their lives.
- Read over the fruit of the Spirit (see Galatians 5:22-23) and the armor of God (see Ephesians 6:10-20) for ideas. Spend some time praying over your list.

Chapter 1

Lord, Give Me Patience

Love Is Patient

You can learn many things from children. How much patience you have, for instance.

—FRANKLIN P. JONES

Having patience is the thing I probably struggle with most as a mom, and this seems to be true for many mothers I talk to. Satan loves to see us lose our cool, especially with our families. It hurts the very ones we love the most and lets him cut to the core of our Christian lives. It can divide our families and keep us from passing on God's truth to the next generation. Proverbs 14:17 says, "A quick-tempered man does foolish things." Losing our patience builds walls between our children and us, walls that can take a long time to tear down. Because we desire to pass patience on as a gift to our children, we must love them as Jesus loves us: just as we are—imperfect.

I remember a difficult time soon after we had moved to a new city. My daughter Sarah was under pressure at her new school. Her young and inexperienced teacher told her to do the month's work her class had done before we moved there, plus her daily lessons. It was too much for any child. When I told her repeatedly to quit working and go to bed, she yelled at me and refused, frustrated because her work wasn't done. I explained that her father and I had scheduled a meeting with her teacher. She angrily insisted she had to do it, even though it was very late and she was tired. Looking back now with more understanding of her personality, I know how important it was to her. But at that moment, I totally lost my patience with her.

Later I hugged her and asked for forgiveness. But the deed was done. I failed Love 101 right when she needed me most.

Sarah forgave me, and God forgave me. But it took time to forgive myself. If you've ever really lost it with your kids, you can relate to my feelings of regret and failure. The move, my husband's travel schedule, and all sorts of pressures had led up to that moment. After the move I had let myself get run down; I wasn't in the Word, hadn't met Christian friends, and had no Christian fellowship. I hadn't guarded my daily walk with God, so I had become vulnerable; I wasn't wearing any armor.

I grew from that experience because God forgives us and teaches us to learn from our mistakes. But I also learned that I would rather work on prevention than endure the pain of recovery.

Here are a dozen ideas for "patience preservation." I'm sure you have some great ideas to add to the list.

- Take care of yourself. Make sure you and your children get enough rest. Even if your preschoolers have outgrown naptime, plan for a quiet time in their rooms every day. Force yourself to sit down and put your feet up during some of that time, no matter what other things need to be done.
- Exercise and eat healthy meals. Encourage those happy endorphins!
- Slow down. Enjoy your kids. Plan ahead to avoid the crisis situations that often result from time crunches.
- Spend time studying the Bible and reading good Christian books on parenting and personal growth. Plan a yearly spiritual retreat for yourself.

- Join a Christian mothers' group for support.
- Build strong friendships with other Christian moms.
- When you sense a buildup of stress, reconsider whatever you're trying to accomplish at the moment in light of the big picture of life. Be flexible. Change your priorities if the pressures on you and your children are too demanding.
- When you feel you're losing your patience with your kids, say, "Mommy needs a moment by herself." Go into another room, take several deep breaths, and pray. Count to twenty before rejoining your family. (Ten isn't enough; your kids can't give you thirty!)
- Try to understand the situation from your children's point of view.
- See Jesus in the faces of your children.
- Remember that whatever you do is to be done with love and with your kids' positive growth as God's children in mind.
- Thank God for his love and patience with you.

Patience really is possible to achieve. We all have the capacity to change and be changed. When we make mistakes, we need to forgive ourselves and keep going. Peter denied Christ three times, but he never gave up on himself. Peter learned from his mistakes and continued on, forgiven, serving Christ.

As mothers, we are on the front line. But we have to take care of ourselves if we want to take care of others.

God's Promises

God is quick to forgive my sins and mistakes. When I ask, he will help me control my anger, teach me to listen well, and give me patience so I can live in a way that pleases him.

> The Lord is compassionate and gracious,
>   slow to anger, abounding in love. . . .

As far as the east is from the west,

> so far has he removed our transgressions from us.
>> (Psalm 103:8,12)

Everyone should be quick to listen, slow to speak and slow to become angry, for man's anger does not bring about the righteous life that God desires. (James 1:19-20)

A Mother's Prayer

Thank you, Lord, for your gracious forgiveness when I lose my patience. Please give me a calm, patient, and loving spirit. Help me slow down and be a good listener. Give me wisdom to understand my own needs and the needs of my children.

Help me teach my children about patience by showing them ways to practice it as a daily habit and by modeling it in my behavior toward them.

Positive Parenting Plans

Spend some time writing down practical ways to nourish yourself so you can be more patient. Consider these ideas as starters:

- Get a great coffee-table book from the library with photos of a place you've always wanted to visit. Browse through it, even if it's late at night.
- Go for a walk.
- Get regular exercise.
- Buy a plant at the supermarket.
- Get a latte at the local bookstore and browse through magazines.
- Exchange e-mail prayer requests with a friend.
- Read an encouraging Christian magazine.
- Memorize James 1:19-20 with your family.

Chapter 2

I Can't Do It All

Love Is Patient

Ruthlessly eliminate hurry from your world.

—DALLAS WILLARD

Incompetence is not a sin; impatience is.

—UNKNOWN

Take a minute to list your five highest priorities as a mother. Now list the five things you really spend most of your time on. Compare the two lists; how well do they match up?

We need to be balanced moms, aware of where we spend our time and energy. Periodically, we need to examine our schedules and adjust them to reflect our real priorities, not the ones put on us by others. This means asking ourselves what God's priorities for us are and, in light of that, what we really want to accomplish. We need to get in the habit of saying to other people, "Let me check my calendar and get back to you."

Time with our children is fleeting (even though certain phases of challenging behavior seem to last forever!). We think we have all the time in the world, but that way of thinking allows us to put off the really important things (read "people") as we use up our time and energy on the daily necessities, such as getting the kids off to school, tackling household chores or work responsibilities, and getting food on the table. Eventually we wake up and realize that we never made time for all those wonderful or important moments we wanted to enjoy with our children "someday."

We need to be on the alert for key words or behaviors that indicate when our children really do need our attention. Some days they're just fine; other days we may need to reevaluate our priorities on an hourly basis. We need to frequently ask ourselves, *Is holding to this particular goal, worthwhile as it may be, causing me to miss an opportunity to communicate God's love?*

Beware of the false guilt that comes from being your own inflexible, goal-driven boss. You are a worthy and loved person whether or not you finish your Bible study, Christmas shopping, cooking, financial planning, or card writing. Yes, we want to live deliberately, but we also need to give ourselves plenty of grace.

With Jesus as our example, the key is focusing on people and things that have eternal value. The Bible says, "Where there is no vision, the people perish" (Proverbs 29:18, KJV). What is your vision for your children? What do you desire to see happen in their lives? One mom shared that before her children were born, she began praying that they would grow up to be a light in the world. She also prayed that they would have a deep hunger for righteousness and for God's Word. Spend some time with your husband talking about the vision you both have for your children and then begin praying specifically for them. When you face a conflict regarding how to use your time, follow your priorities.

If the house is a little messy or you don't return a few calls right away because you're spending time with your son or daughter, then you have used your time well. Whether it's making time for meaningful conversations about Jesus, addressing the stressful issues in your children's lives, or getting down on your knees to help build a pretend store with a bedsheet for a roof, make each moment count.

▌ God's Promises

My life will be well spent if I love God and other people and plan to make these two things my top priorities.

> "The most important [commandment] . . . is this: '. . . Love the Lord your God with all your heart and with all your soul and with all your mind and with all your strength.' The second is this: 'Love your neighbor as yourself.' There is no commandment greater than these." (Mark 12:29-31)

> And what does the Lord require of you?
> To act justly and to love mercy
>   and to walk humbly with your God. (Micah 6:8)

> Where there is no vision, the people perish. (Proverbs 29:18, KJV)

A Mother's Prayer

Lord, please give me insight into the hearts of my children. Give me your vision for their lives and show me how to pray for them more specifically.

Please make my children's hearts tender about the things that really matter. Help me teach them, through words and example, that people are more important than material things. May they love you and act justly, love mercy, and walk humbly with you all their lives.

Positive Parenting Plans

- Write out a plan to organize just one area of your life in order to make things easier for yourself. This could be as simple as clearing off the table beside your bed or as complex as reprioritizing your weekly schedule.

- Read a little booklet called *Tyranny of the Urgent*, published by InterVarsity Press, in which author Charles Hummel writes about how to discern what is really important in a day from what is merely making the most noise.
- Create a "life prayer list" for each of your children, addressing any needs or concerns specific to each child's personality and development. Keep the lists in a special place and add to them as you and your family grow and change.

Chapter 3

It Takes a Family

Love Is Patient

It's not that you arrive at a certain point; you never arrive at a finish line in a relationship. Instead, you constantly change and grow, stretch and squirm.
—DANN HUFF, MUSICIAN

Parenting is not a one-person job—at least not if you want to maintain your sanity. It's important to nurture your children's relationships with other family members who can help shape their lives and faith for the better.

I've been blessed to have the love of my husband for over forty years. He's a man who loves God and kids. One of the things that first attracted me to him was the way he loved and played with his young nieces and nephews. In every way, he has been a true partner in the raising of our children and the spoiling of our grandchildren.

When our kids were young, he traveled quite a lot. Because of that, I had to make sure to step back and encourage his relationship with the kids when he returned. But whether he was home or away, he was always 100 percent available to them. The kids had his office number and later his cell phone number, and we always knew that he would answer our calls anytime, even if he was in a meeting.

He made the kids feel secure and loved. He would wrestle with, tickle, and do crazy stunts with them. He even helped one of our daughters pick out her prom dress when I was in the hospital. She still laughs about the look on his face at some of the dresses she tried on.

The two of us are total opposites in many ways. Like most people, we have had to work to make our marriage a good one. We had to put Christ at the center of our relationship. I had to make sure that my role as a mom never became more important than my role as a wife, which is to love, honor, and respect my husband.

Having a good marriage is another book in itself, but there are plenty of good Christian books on marriage out there. I simply want to encourage you to cherish your husband as your mate and to value the important role fathers play within the family. Your children are learning about parenting and marriage by watching how you interact with their dad.

If you are raising children without a husband in the home, whatever the circumstances, it is a tough road to go alone. Look for a good, trustworthy Christian man to be involved with your kids, someone who will be there over the long haul. Whether he is an uncle or a grandfather or a longtime trusted family friend, kids need to have a male in a positive, nurturing role.

Children also benefit from positive relationships with extended family members, especially their grandparents. After we marry and have children, our relationship with our parents changes. We may have different parenting techniques and lifestyle choices. We need to respect their advice but go in the direction God leads us as parents. We can plan opportunities for fun times together that give our parents a chance to get to know and love their grandchildren, and we can suggest ways to strengthen their relationship. Phone calls, e-mails, postcards, and letters can help keep the connection strong between visits. It's also important to balance sharing holidays and special times with both sets of grandparents, but be sure to protect opportunities to build traditions within your own family as well.

That brings up another important relationship in families: in-laws, especially mothers-in-law, who have become the subject of many bad jokes over the years. Guess what? When our kids get married, we all become mothers-in-law. What a change that makes in our perspective!

My mother-in-law is with the Lord now, and I'm sure she is happily organizing heaven and cooking up some fabulous southern meals for everyone. Her "love language" was food. She loved to cook huge meals. She raised a large family in some difficult situations, and I'm sure she felt she had done her best if she could at least send them out into their day with a full stomach. She canned, made fabulous pickles, and kept an immaculate home.

Then she got me as a daughter-in-law. We were very different people, and it took us several years to really feel at peace with each other. We had to work hard in our relationship to accommodate different points of view about nearly everything, from where our wedding would be held to child rearing. Differences between generations added to the misunderstandings. By the grace of God, we learned to treat each other with honesty and love. She relaxed after a few years and realized I would (probably!) not kill her youngest son with my cooking and laissez-faire housekeeping. When our children came along, she and my father-in-law were good grandparents.

I learned to assume that her motivation was love and to look at the positive things she contributed, especially to our children. I also learned to stand up for the decisions my husband and I made as a couple in the way we raised our children. I discovered the importance of forgiving, keeping short accounts, and avoiding certain topics of discussion in which our differences would never be resolved. I strived to be respectful and keep the relationship healthy for my husband's and children's sake.

I now have the wonderful added relationship of a son-in-law—or, as we say, "son-in-love"—whom we're crazy about. Because we raised daughters, I don't have any script to go by in this new relationship (and neither does he). I'm learning to be teachable, becoming a student not only of my kids and my husband but also of my other important family relationships.

Our kids need as many loving adults as possible to rely on in their growing-up years. And so do we. So let's work on keeping our relationships strong and healthy and pleasing to God.

God's Promises

I please God by making my love for others my first concern.

> You, my [sisters], were called to be free. But do not use your freedom to indulge the sinful nature; rather, serve one another in love. The entire law is summed up in a single command: "Love your neighbor as yourself." (Galatians 5:13-14)

> A patient [woman] has great understanding,
>   but a quick-tempered [woman] displays folly.
>   (Proverbs 14:29)

> A gentle answer turns away wrath,
>   but a harsh word stirs up anger. (Proverbs 15:1)

A Mother's Prayer

Dear God, thank you for my husband. Please help me love and respect him. Let us find opportunities for special times together both as a family and as a couple. Please give me understanding, love, and respect for the other people in my family as well. Let them see Jesus in me. Give me patience and love for my in-laws, even if we are very different.

Help me assume the best in their motives and appreciate the good things they add to our family, especially to our children. Help me weigh the advice of others but be confident in the parenting decisions I have learned from you.

Please give my children respect for their elders. I pray that they will love, honor, and respect my husband and me and their grandparents as long as they live. I pray that they will learn much about family relationships and Christian love so that one day they can have strong Christian families of their own. Please help me teach them the value of servanthood and selflessness.

Positive Parenting Plans

- Make a special effort to keep your children in touch with your parents and in-laws. Depending on their age, help them do what they can on their own to keep in regular contact. Send photos, artwork, and reports on their activities regularly.

- Help your children plan special one-on-one times with Daddy, such as an afternoon together at a ball game or the park or even just working together in the yard.

Chapter 4

How Should I Spend My Life?

Love Is Patient

Time is the coin of your life. It is the only coin you have, and only you can determine how it will be spent. Be careful lest you let other people spend it for you.
— CARL SANDBURG

How we spend our days is, of course, how we spend our lives.
— ANNIE DILLARD, *AN AMERICAN CHILDHOOD*

Several years ago a movie made popular the Latin phrase *carpe diem*, meaning "seize the day." It appeared on coffee mugs and T-shirts everywhere. For moms, the days either fly too fast or crawl too slowly. There doesn't seem to be a middle ground. We're either wishing that the day were over or that it would never end. Our time with our kids is a fleeting and precious gift, but sometimes it seems as though we're in such a hurry. None of us knows the amount of time our children or we have been given. It's not something to be afraid of or worried about, but it is important to value our time and make the most of it. We want to seize each day and squeeze out of it all the good we can.

As Christians and as moms, we want to live a life that pleases God, yet sometimes we aren't sure how that desire can shape our day-to-day choices. With a sink full of dirty dishes, piles of laundry to fold, and little voices crying for attention, we may sometimes feel as if we have no choice about how our time is spent. And yet each day is packed with twenty-four hours' worth of opportunity to invest our lives in something worthwhile.

I have learned that understanding God's will for my life gives me a good picture of how he wants me to spend my days. He created me and gave me certain talents, desires, and interests. He did the same for my children. That knowledge can direct the way I spend my time. God gives us such freedom that the only limits on the way I use my days are my choices, my present circumstances, the strength of my will, the breadth of my vision, and the depth of my understanding of his will for my life.

God has definite desires for the outcome of our lives and a plan for the best way for us to spend our days. Our children belong to him too, so as we plan how to use our time, we must consider what God wants us to accomplish with our children's lives as well as our own. Here are some ways you can help your children spend their coins of life well. Add your own thoughts that reflect the unique goals of your family.

- Introduce them to God.
- Help them learn to spend time on things of value.
- Involve them in serving others.
- Help them begin to build their character by introducing values such as compassion, self-discipline, thankfulness, joy, responsibility, generosity, and perseverance.
- Affirm their worth, value, and significance. Point out the things that are beautiful and strong about them.
- Introduce them to worthwhile books and stories that have adventures, heroic deeds, and art—tales that teach them the funny side of life, that broaden their worldview and their under-

standing of human nature, and that teach them about God's love and power and saving grace.

- Severely limit TV, video games, and mindless computer use—the great suckers of life, time, and brainpower.
- Teach them to dream big dreams and tell them that dreams can come true.
- Listen to and talk with them.
- Love them and teach them about joy.

While making the care of our children a priority, we shortchange them if we don't also seek opportunities for our own personal growth. Our children need to witness a balance of caring for others without neglecting self. Don't worry about measuring up to the standards of someone else, such as the often-mentioned Proverbs 31 woman. This passage presents an idealized picture of a wealthy woman with servants using her time well in a different century, not an itemized schedule of how we're to spend our days. Beware of overloading yourself. Leave room for joy.

Here are some ideas of what you can do to best spend your time during this season of your life.

- Invest in Bible study and quiet time with God.
- Journal to get a better understanding of who you are and what your strengths and weaknesses are.
- Dream personal dreams and model for your kids that dreams can come true.
- Improve your work skills for your personal satisfaction and for additional provision for your family, if necessary.
- Read good books to keep in touch with the world, to improve your mind and skills, or to simply relax.
- Listen to and talk with your husband and work to keep your love strong, for now and for when you have an empty nest.

- Volunteer service to others in a way that fits your gifts and gives you joy and personal satisfaction.
- Join an exercise class, gym, or small group to keep physically fit.
- Value and enjoy old friendships and make new ones.
- Love and encourage people in your home or in another city or country.
- Learn to say no to things that suck time or don't fit your priorities, and leave room for the unexpected serendipity of life. Some of the best things in life are unplanned.

Life is made up of different seasons. In this season when our children are living at home, there are many things clamoring for our time. There's no magic formula or plan to fit every family. We just need to make wise choices that line up with our priorities—and be sure to match our priorities up with God's. We all have different hopes and wonderful dreams for our children and for ourselves. To make those dreams come true, we need to spend time in prayer before we spend our time.

God's Promises

God gives me all the time I need for the things he wants me to accomplish.

> There is a time for everything,
> and a season for every activity under heaven. (Ecclesiastes 3:1)

> Teach us to make the most of our time,
> so that we may grow in wisdom. (Psalm 90:12, NLT)

A Mother's Prayer

Thank you for my life and for all the choices I have in which to spend it. Please give me wisdom and discernment every day as I make choices about using my time. Help me

*take the pressures of time off the shoulders of my children and relax and enjoy them
instead of hurrying them.*

*I ask that my children will acknowledge your perfect will and walk in it through-
out their lives. I ask also that as they do that, they will live joyful and worthy lives with
time for dreaming big dreams, investing in good works, and bearing good fruit.*

Positive Parenting Plans

- Sit down with your husband at least four times a year and make
  family plans. Examine your schedules and make sure they fit
  with the long-term vision and priorities you have for your family.
  This is a good time to plan vacations for the family and getaways
  for the two of you.
- Establish two or more TV-free nights per week and use that
  time for a fun family activity or project, such as building something together or reading a book as a family.
- Read *Margin* by Richard Swenson (published by NavPress) to get
  excellent ideas for restoring time reserves to overloaded families.

Chapter 5

Being the Grown-Up

Love Is Kind

Being considerate of the feelings and needs of others by exhibiting gentleness shows you are responding to the Spirit of God.
—Stormie Omartian, *The Power of a Praying Woman*

One of the big issues in life for me is growing up versus just growing older. Not all people learn the difference. A big part of maturing as a Christian is learning to put the needs of others before our own and being kind and gentle while we do it. It's part of that servanthood thing that Jesus was always talking about and demonstrating in his life. And being a mom is a crash course in servanthood.

It's not always easy to be kind to our children. We get worn down by their needs and frustrated by their behavior. They can make a walk to the car last all day. Kids take three times as long as we would to do just about everything. But children are not small adults. They think differently. Their priorities and skills are different from ours. When our children are frustrating our purposes and plans, we sometimes find ourselves thinking, *Hey, I'm the person in charge here. You have to do what I want, not vice versa.* But Jesus was the person in charge in a way that really mattered. And he never once misused his infinite power. He was kind to those around him, putting their needs first. He even washed their smelly, dung-encrusted feet. And you thought your kids' feet got dirty!

Children are so beautiful, like varied flowers in a garden. They come in many shapes, sizes, and colors. Some grow fast, and some take their time; they all grow and bloom in their own unique way. Like a gifted gardener, a mother's role in nurturing her children is both difficult and delightful. Sometimes we get to enjoy beauty and sweet fragrance, and other times we're sweating and pulling weeds in the heat of the day.

Moms and daughters go through some difficult things that dads and daughters seem to avoid. I remember when one of my adolescent daughters was going through a stage where she argued with everything I said. To test this theory one day as we were driving, I mentioned that the sky was really blue that day; she insisted that it was gray. There were few ways we could relate. Already drained from the demands of a full-time job, I found myself losing my patience with her on our daily drive to school. After I prayed over a very hard day of butting heads with her, God gave me the wisdom to see that she really was unable to break the pattern of her rebellious attitude. The hormonal and emotional changes of passing from childhood to adulthood made it impossible for her to think clearly at that time. So it was up to me—the grown-up—to restore our relationship.

I decided to take my adult expectations off of her, accept her, and treat her with kindness and love. She was still my cherished and tender daughter, hidden underneath this new attitude. My change in perspective took the edge off my responses and allowed me to meet her testing attitude with love. Previously, my message conveyed that I couldn't love and accept her unless she was performing well. As my attitude and tone of voice changed, she felt safe and loved, and our times together began to be special again.

Kids do grow up. They won't always need so much of your time and energy. You won't always be the center of their universe. But you'll always be part of their definition of home. In the meantime, being "kind to one another, tenderhearted, forgiving one another" (Ephesians 4:32, NKJV) needs to be reflected in our words and actions to our family. And hopefully someday that lovingkindness will come back to us from our grown-up children.

God's Promises

Words and acts of love hold more power than demanding control or using heavy-handed authority.

> Pleasant words are a honeycomb,
> > sweet to the soul and healing to the bones. (Proverbs 16:24)

> Most important of all, continue to show deep love for each other, for love covers a multitude of sins. (1 Peter 4:8, NLT)

A Mother's Prayer

Dear God, please help me understand my children's hearts. Give me a servant's heart, insight, and creative inspiration for showing love in meaningful ways. Let my words be like a healing balm in our family relationships.

Please grow the character traits of kindness and generosity in my children. Let their words be those that build others up.

Positive Parenting Plans

- Write down some really great things about being a mom and thank God for them. Write down some really great things about your kids and thank God for them.
- Study to understand your kids and the changes and stresses they are facing. Their world is constantly changing, inside and out. There are excellent books on the different stages and ages, but use your God-given "mom sense" too.

Chapter 6

Feeling Valued

Love Is Kind

A three-year-old child is a being who gets almost as much fun out of a fifty-six dollar set of swings as it does out of a small green worm.

—BILL VAUGHN

What do children value? If you look at the treasures they carry in their pockets or keep in their special place, you may smile and cry tears of tenderness at the same time. A bird's feather, slightly crumpled. A few stones of different colors and shapes. A plastic worm. A ragged doll or stuffed animal with all the fuzz worn off. One small friend of mine carried a small strip of cloth with three strings hanging down from it; it was the remains of her mother's baby blanket after two generations of washings and adventures. My grandson loved a small, once blue, wobbly-headed toy dinosaur that was absolutely threadbare.

But I have found that the things children value the most are intangible. Time with you is the biggest, most priceless treasure your children can have. If they could put it in their pocket to pull out whenever they needed it, they would guard it with their lives. While it may not always be easy or convenient, making the effort to include our children in even the most mundane of daily tasks—grocery shopping, cooking, and cleaning, for example—helps satisfy their hunger to be included, to know they are wanted and needed.

You have countless other opportunities throughout each day to nurture your children's sense of belonging. Your smile, directed at them in a megawatt "love beam." The words you say to affirm their worth and value, such as "Wow, you're really smart. You figured out how to do that" or "I love you so much. I'm so glad God gave you to me." Loving words are worth their weight in diamonds. So is a loving touch—patting a head, giving a hug, swinging them into your arms for a tickle or a cuddle. Even when they're older and so much "cooler," although they may not voice it, they still want to be hugged and made to feel special. Teen years can be lonely.

When we speak to our children, we want to give them words to treasure, words that communicate love and build them up, because some of these words will stay with them forever. When I reflect back on my childhood, I can remember things said to me over thirty years ago. I remember both the unkind things and the loving things vividly. Some of the endearments and pet names I called my children were passed down from my parents and on to my grandchildren. I can still remember my mother coming sleepily downstairs to my bedroom on a cold winter night when I was sure scary things were lurking in my closet or under my bed. Her words of reassurance made everything all right with my world and let me fall asleep. Then she dragged herself tiredly back to bed after she had given me the treasure of security.

Our words, actions, and attitudes continually demonstrate what it is that we most value, where our deepest priorities lie. If we truly believe that people are more important than things or money, this will be reflected in our daily choices—and eventually bear fruit in the lives of our children. As we love our children and share in every possible way the message that God loves them, we are building a strong net of security under them for the days when the world will whisper that they have no worth. So let's focus on the good things they do. Let's reassure them that even when we aren't with them, God is.

Don't let a day pass by without saying "I love you" to your children in some way. They are our treasures.

God's Promises

My choices reveal what I treasure and where my heart is. If I love others, God's love is made complete in me.

> "Where your treasure is, there your heart will be also."
> (Matthew 6:21, NKJV)

> No one has ever seen God; but if we love one another,
> God lives in us and his love is made complete in us.
> (1 John 4:12)

> Be imitators of God, therefore, as dearly loved children
> and live a life of love, just as Christ loved us and gave himself up for us as a fragrant offering and sacrifice to God.
> (Ephesians 5:1-2)

A Mother's Prayer

Thank you for valuing me so much that you gave your Son's life for mine. Lord, help me love and treasure my children. I ask that your love will be very real to them and that they will learn to trust you at each stage in their lives. Please help me teach them to treasure people over things and to invest their lives in what truly matters.

Positive Parenting Plans

- Plan some activities this week for you and your children where there are no distractions or lines to wait in. Maybe it's as simple as going for a walk together. Really listen to them and encourage them.
- Spend some time praying through and updating your life prayer lists for your children.

Chapter 7

Father, Give Us Thankful Hearts

Love Does Not Envy

Only he who gives thanks for little things receives the big things.
—DIETRICH BONHOEFFER, *LIFE TOGETHER*

I love giving gifts to my young grandchildren. But I notice that if I do it too often, they begin to look for the gift when I visit instead of just being glad to see me and get a hug. Ever notice that when you take your kids somewhere really special, such as the zoo or an amusement park, they become focused on what to do next or what to eat or the special souvenir they "need" to buy rather than simply having fun with you? Aren't we like that with God sometimes? He blesses us, and we go right on to the next thing we want from him. We forget that his loving presence is enough.

We so easily overlook the many good things in our lives because we get caught up in chasing after what we don't have or because we're measuring ourselves against what others have. Our culture teaches us to constantly compare ourselves with others. Advertising and marketing campaigns foster discontent—enticing us with more, better, newer, different, bigger—so we will spend money. But there's never an end to it.

I have a lovely kitchen, but all the appliances are white. Now the magazines and decorating shows are saying appliances need to be stainless steel. I find myself looking at my perfectly good dishwasher and oven and thinking I need new ones, instead of sending money to help those who don't have a house with electricity or plumbing.

Proverbs 14:30 says,

> A heart at peace gives life to the body,
>   but envy rots the bones.

Envy is Satan's sneaky way of taking our eyes off all the blessings we have been given. Instead of being genuinely happy for someone else, a little voice whispers that we should have the same good fortune. Money, and all the things it buys, can cause us to envy. Good looks and good health, job opportunities, and God-given abilities and talents can prompt envy, even of our friends.

We envy not only for ourselves. We may also envy for our children. If we work outside the home, we envy the mother who gets to stay with her children instead of entrusting them to child care, especially in the summers. We may envy families who can afford to dress their children in the latest fashions or whose financial success grants opportunities for recreation, camps, and educational programs. We may ruefully compare our children to those who easily earn good grades or who excel at athletics or have healthier bodies. Our attitudes can even affect our relationships with our children, who may not feel good enough. And they will certainly pick up our feelings of discontent.

The main thing envy does is take our eyes off of the ways God *has* provided for us. We become like Adam and Eve or the Israelites, always complaining and looking at what they did not have. Don't we hate that attitude when we see it in our children? How much God must hate it when he sees it in us.

My ninety-year-old neighbor is a wonder. Every fall, she and her granddaughter begin collecting things for the Christmas shoebox ministry of Operation Christmas Child. They save toys, money, and boxes and then go shopping together. On a Saturday, they wrap everything and take it to their church. Over the years, that young girl has learned how to be generous. Now, as a teenager, she is more attuned to the needs of others and not so easily self-absorbed.

As moms we can help our kids learn compassion. We can show them how to be joyful, thankful, and content. Let's pledge to tune out the shouts of our culture for more, bigger, and newer. Let's pray for protection from greed and envy for ourselves and our families. Let's thank our generous God for all the blessings he has already showered on us and be joyful just to be in his presence.

■ God's Promises

If my children and I give thanks in all situations, pray, and use our gifts for other people, we will live a life of joy and contentment.

> Each one should use whatever gift he has received to serve others, faithfully administering God's grace in its various forms. (1 Peter 4:10)

> Be joyful always; pray continually; give thanks in all circumstances, for this is God's will for you in Christ Jesus. (1 Thessalonians 5:16-18)

> A heart at peace gives life to the body,
> but envy rots the bones. (Proverbs 14:30)

A Mother's Prayer

Father, please forgive me for any envious and ungrateful thoughts I have had. Give me a spirit that rejoices when others receive blessings.

Thank you for all the gifts and talents you have given my children and me. Please give me wisdom in helping develop them. Please show us how to use those talents for the good of others and to reflect honor back to you. Please give my children and me generous spirits and thankful hearts.

Positive Parenting Plans

- Look around your community for a chance to serve with your children.
- Check out www.samaritanspurse.org to learn more about Operation Christmas Child. Get your children involved in filling up a shoebox to help demonstrate God's love to others.
- Be a "secret Santa" to someone in need.
- During the year find ways to help less fortunate kids in your town.
- If your children are older, learn how to raise support so they can go on a missions trip.

Chapter 8

Finding My Own Style

Love Does Not Envy

Do not wish to be anything but what you are.
—SAINT FRANCIS DE SALES

God made each of us different. He gave us different talents and abilities, different bents and interests, different personalities and faces, different bodies and minds. So why should we expect everyone to mother the same? Have you given any thought to what kind of mother you are? Have you found your own groove, your own style? And are you content with being who you are?

There are as many different family lifestyles as there are mothers. Let me tell you about a few mothers I know who approach motherhood in very different ways.

Let's start with Lisa. This very intelligent woman wanted a career. Then she was struck by lightning in the form of a guy named Kevin. They fell in love and got married. She worked for a while, and then she got pregnant. Now they have three wonderful children, all under age six and very much loved. All the energy Lisa once focused on work she now invests in her family. Along with her husband, she has established strict but fair rules for the children to follow. She breastfeeds. She homeschools. She makes her own bread, butter, and preserves. She plans, cooks, and freezes organic meals for two weeks at a time, plus makes extra to take to friends who have new babies or other needs in their lives. She sews clever dress-up outfits and trick-or-treat costumes for her kids and makes her own curtains. She lives in a house that she and her husband totally remade with the help of friends. A dynamo of energy, she has painted, stripped wallpaper, and replaced tile and carpet to create a home she enjoys. She teaches at church twice a month, and her family supports several ministries with time and money. Lisa is a warm and loving mother and friend. She loves the Lord. She is a terrific mom.

Then there is Alysha. She fell in love with a guy who didn't want the responsibility of a family. She is a single mom who works five days a week. She has one child whom she drops off and picks up at a church preschool and daycare center. She buys takeout often and has pizza night every Friday. She's learning to use a Crock-Pot. Her son has a few rules to follow. She prays, plays, and sings with him at the dinner table. Sometimes she does church at home because she doesn't want to leave her child in another classroom. She sits down and plays with him every night after a long day at work and then reads stories they've picked out at the library until he falls asleep. Sometimes she falls asleep with him. She buys most of his clothes and toys at garage sales. She takes him for special weekend outings to the zoo or on bike rides or even skiing when she can afford it. She supports an old friend in a ministry to China. Alysha is a warm and loving mother and friend. She loves the Lord. She is a terrific mom.

Next is Nicci. She and her husband tried for years to have children and finally adopted two beautiful kids. She quit her job to stay at home with them. Perhaps because of their perspective as older parents, Nicci and her husband have a fairly casual and relaxed household. She likes to give her kids and their friends treats and sugary drinks. Her kids have very few rules to follow. Money is not a problem. The couple buys lots of great toys, and they're planning to put a swimming pool in their backyard when the kids get older. She has a housekeeper come in twice a month. She is a great cook. She takes her kids to church every Sunday and brings lots of treats for the class. She spends a great deal of her time driving her kids to dance and athletic practices because every season they're in a different sport. She often takes her children to special events for kids in the region. She volunteers with her husband and kids at a ministry, serving meals to street people. Nicci is a warm and loving mother and friend. She loves the Lord. She is a terrific mom.

Believe me, although each of these women has her own style of child rearing and living, you would like every one of them. Yet as you read their descriptions, did you find yourself judging them, perhaps comparing them to each other—or to yourself? Did you feel uncomfortable with some of their priorities or choices? If so, that's natural because you are a different person in different circumstances and with a different personality. The only "right" way for you to mother is the way in which God has called and equipped you.

So how would you describe yourself to someone who has never met you? Would you say that you are fearfully and wonderfully made by the God who made the universe? You are. Would you say that God is working to make you perfect and complete? He is. Would you say that you are a pretty good mom? You are! Would you say that you have many gifts that you can use to make a difference in the world? You do. So do I, and so do Lisa, Alysha, Nicci, and all the other terrific moms on this planet who know Jesus or will come to know him.

God's Promises

God has made me beautiful and unique and with wonderful gifts so I can be a blessing to others.

So in Christ we who are many form one body, and each member belongs to all the others. We have different gifts, according to the grace given us. (Romans 12:5-6)

Being confident of this, that he who began a good work in you will carry it on to completion until the day of Christ Jesus. (Philippians 1:6)

I praise you because I am fearfully and wonderfully made;
> your works are wonderful,
>> I know that full well. (Psalm 139:14)

And God is able to make all grace abound to you, so that in all things at all times, having all that you need, you will abound in every good work. (2 Corinthians 9:8)

A Mother's Prayer

Dear God, I thank you that I was made by you to be a unique person with my own gifts and style of doing things. Thank you that you won't quit molding and improving me until I am beautiful like Jesus Christ. Thank you for equipping me for doing good works in this world, which certainly means you will help me be a terrific mom.

Please walk with each of my children. Help them see their own beauty and gifts that come from you and use them for others. Help them avoid comparing themselves with anyone but Christ as they seek to become more like him.

Positive Parenting Plans

- Do you know what your gifts and strengths are? Find out. Look for a good study on gifts online or at your Christian bookstore. List what you are good at and what type of service gives you joy and comes easily and naturally to you.

- Help your children discern their strengths and then help them find opportunities to build on them. Is one of them athletic? Find a sport he can enjoy and do well at and then practice with him. Do you have an artistic child? Give her lots of paper, paint, markers, colored pencils, and a place where she can be messy. Is one of your children good at math and building and taking things apart? Get him some gears and building toys.
- Do the same with character traits. Study your children. Get a list of character traits you would like to teach them. Give them opportunities to serve others. Help them be diligent and finish what they start. Help them learn to be orderly in their rooms and play areas.

Chapter 9

Changing Priorities

Love Is Not Proud

Humility, that low, sweet root from which all heavenly virtues shoot.
—THOMAS MOORE, "THE LOVES OF THE ANGELS"

Motherhood is a humbling experience from the very beginning. Over a period of nine months, we grow out of all our favorite clothes, and our shape becomes unrecognizable. Then we're naked before several strangers in green masks while we birth our babies. After that, if we make the decision to give up our jobs in the world, be they ever so humble or great, we give up one of the things that defines us. Instead of a teacher or marketing manager, we become simply Jordan's mommy or Michaela's mother. It's a humbling experience that few husbands can relate to.

Many mothers find this transition very difficult. At first we try to do it all perfectly—maintain a spotless house, follow the parenting books to the letter, keep our children and ourselves looking good. Then we slowly learn to put our children's needs before our pride and natural inclinations. The house becomes less neat. The cereal dried on the rug becomes like cement. Our shirts become stained with tears, milk, and spit-up. But we are happy because we have happy kids.

In our new role, we have to learn to play again. Some of us feel awkward and self-conscious getting down on the floor and playing with our children; we'd rather supervise from a comfortable distance. We can buy their clothes, bathe them, and read to them, but getting muddy or pretending to be a pet cat or their horse or a customer for their store is humbling and difficult for many of us, especially when we have many other things we want to get done. But playtime deserves a top slot on our to-do list; our children desperately need us to play with them, to wrestle and tickle and be silly with them. They just want us to be there.

Another way our pride takes a beating is when we let the behavior of our children define our worth. When one of our children throws a tantrum, we may be more concerned with what others are thinking of our mothering skills than about what is bothering our child. We may wrongly rush to spank her or hustle her quickly out of sight.

I can still see the looks from strangers as my tired children howled in the grocery cart. I also remember visiting a relative in California and having to run into a discount store to find a cheap outfit for one tear-stained young daughter whose bout with diarrhea had made a mess of her and the one extra outfit I'd brought along on the day trip.

So where should our sense of self and self-esteem come from during these mothering years? We must look to God for approval. He alone knows the patience it takes to clean out with a toothpick the Play-Doh hair from the little plastic head so our child can give another pretend haircut. He witnesses our tenderness in changing dirty diapers, our sacrifice of much-needed sleep, our joy in preparing a child's favorite treat, our faithfulness in accepting the huge responsibility of caring for vulnerable human beings. He alone sees the growth in our character—and he smiles. God sees it all and is proud of us.

Our priorities inevitably change as we begin to get a handle on this mothering thing. Instead of a perfectly clean house, a well-managed project, and a nice paycheck, we look for happy children, a funny art project taped to the fridge, the smell of peanut butter cookies, and the sound of laughter echoing from the kitchen.

God says his greatest priority is love. So if our home is filled with love, the cereal stuck like concrete to the rug doesn't matter. We can cut it out later.

God's Promises

I am the chosen, holy, and dearly loved daughter of God, who uses humbling experiences to shape my character.

> Therefore, as God's chosen people, holy and dearly loved, clothe yourselves with compassion, kindness, humility, gentleness and patience. Bear with each other and forgive whatever grievances you may have against one another. Forgive as the Lord forgave you. And over all these virtues put on love, which binds them all together in perfect unity. (Colossians 3:12-14)

> And [Jesus] said: "I tell you the truth, unless you change and become like little children, you will never enter the kingdom of heaven. Therefore, whoever humbles himself like this child is the greatest in the kingdom of heaven.
>
> "And whoever welcomes a little child like this in my name welcomes me." (Matthew 18:3-5)

> [The Lord] gives grace to the humble. (Proverbs 3:34)

A Mother's Prayer

Dear Father God, please give me a solid anchor of self-esteem in knowing that you created me uniquely and you love me totally, just the way I am. Thank you that there is nothing I must do to make you love me more than you do right now. Please fill me with childlike joy and faith.

Please give my children strong self-esteems based on your love and humble spirits that reflect gratitude and glory back to you for all their talents and abilities.

Positive Parenting Plans

- Add to your children's life prayer lists. Start one for yourself, asking God for a vision of what he wants your life to look like.
- Call 1-800-691-PRAY and ask for a free bookmark called "31 Biblical Virtues to Pray for Your Kids" by Bob Hostetler, or print it off the Internet at www.prayertower.net/Pray4Virtue.htm.

Chapter 10

What Would Miss Manners Do?

Love Is Not Rude

And now I will show you the most excellent way.
If I speak in the tongues of men and of angels, but have not love,
I am only a resounding gong or a clanging cymbal.

—1 CORINTHIANS 12:31–13:1

Feeling snippety? Snapping at others? When at my best, I am not a rude or self-seeking person. But if you catch me when I'm tired, pressured for time, hungry, or depressed—well, let's just say it's not a pretty picture.

When life presses in on us, it can squeeze out our good intentions like a python squeezing life out of its prey. How quickly we let our sin nature take over. Just get in the car and wait until someone cuts you off. And how about that rush to get everyone ready and out the door for church on Sunday morning? Lots of interesting scenes there too.

Too often, our family takes the brunt of our rudeness. Ever been "talking nice" over the phone while shooting dirty looks at your children? Ever snap at your husband in a tone you would never use with your best girlfriend? No, me neither! And I have certainly never yelled at my kids just because their neediness coincided with a moment when I had something more important that I wanted to do. How about that hour when you're trying to get dinner ready but Daddy's not home to help out with the hungry, cranky, clingy kids? Let's be honest—we all lose it. The constant demands of motherhood, with hormone-charged teenagers or toddlers who scream when you try to go to the bathroom in privacy, can prompt even the most well-intentioned mom to say things that wound her children.

I remember asking my kids when they were (occasionally) rude teenagers to please treat me with at least the same respect they gave their friends and telling them that I would try to do the same. Common politeness and good manners can go a long way in oiling the screechy wheel of family relationships.

How do we minimize our own rude and selfish behavior, not to mention set a good example for our children? "Do as I say, not as I do" doesn't work. The opposite is nearly always true.

First of all, we must decide to change. We need to honestly view our behavior as sin and ask God to help us recognize immediately when we're slipping into rude behavior or a self-seeking attitude. He can replace a bad attitude with a joyful, generous, thankful spirit.

Surprisingly, when we're feeling selfish and rude, one of the best things we can do is serve someone else with generosity and encouragement. It makes us feel good and surprises the other person. One mother I know uses "forced acts of kindness" to conquer "random acts of rudeness." When one of her boys is rude to the other, she requires him to perform an act of kindness for his brother. This works for adults too.

In addition to having a willing, teachable spirit, we can do some practical preventative work. Often we sort of realize we're "moms behaving badly," but we just can't think reasonably enough to stop ourselves. Here are some tools that, when put into practice, can help you break the pattern of losing it with your children. I'm sure you have some good ideas to add.

- Spend time in God's Word. Memorize and post a few key positive verses where you'll see them often.
- Share your struggles with a trusted prayer partner.
- Keep a flexible schedule to avoid time pressures.
- Discover your limits—and your children's. There are only so many things that can be done in a day without causing meltdowns.
- Learn to say no. This is a powerful tool!
- Build some God time, personal time, and rest time into your life.

The big key for women is to realize that we are emotional creatures. That's a good thing. It's what helps us discern needs in others and empathize with them. It's what equips us to love so well. But it's also why little things can set us off center, why our feelings get hurt, and why we can get in a mood. We need to be sensitive to recognize our attitudes and mood swings, do what we can to prevent them, and prepare to dig ourselves out of them with God's help. We can go to the Well to refill our cup of joy.

God's Promises

My words become beautiful when spoken with love. God offers me the strength and grace I need to put others first, even when life is difficult.

A word aptly spoken
   is like apples of gold in settings of silver. (Proverbs 25:11)

[Love] is not rude, it is not self-seeking, it is not easily angered, it keeps no record of wrongs. (1 Corinthians 13:5)

When I was a child, I talked like a child, I thought like a child, I reasoned like a child. [But now], I put childish ways behind me. (1 Corinthians 13:11)

Be devoted to one another in brotherly love. Honor one
another above yourselves. (Romans 12:10)

A Mother's Prayer

Please keep me from wallowing in bad moods and mood swings. Help me recognize and prevent them. Thank you that I am an emotional woman capable of deep feelings of empathy, love, and joy. But instead of letting my emotions control me, I ask for an abundance of your grace and peace so that I may live with a steady, joyful, and generous spirit.

I pray that you would fill my children with the assurance that they are greatly loved, by me and by you. Please give them hearts full of compassion and the knowledge that joy comes in serving others.

Positive Parenting Plans

- Make your own list of ways to avoid stressful situations where you'll blow your cool.
- Plan as a family to surprise someone else with a random act of kindness.
- Memorize Romans 12:10.
- Do something nice and relaxing for yourself.

Chapter 11

When Momma Ain't Happy

Love Is Not Self-Seeking

*Here's the truth: when Mama ain't happy, it's Mama's responsibility
to deal with it.*

—CAROL KUYKENDALL, MOPS INTERNATIONAL

You've surely seen or heard—or perhaps even have posted in your
kitchen—the semi-humorous saying "When Mama ain't happy, ain't
nobody happy." As moms, we have the opportunity to set the tone in the
house. But it's not always easy to maintain a consistently joyful spirit.

When my children were small, I left behind an interesting job to
plunge into the less than glamorous world of wiping bottoms, cleaning
Cheerios off chairs, and completing countless chores—only to do them
again, day after day.

The trade-off was definitely worth it; I would still make that same
choice today. I treasure my wonderful grown children and young grandchildren. However, I wish I would've understood more fully at the time
the vital importance and privilege of being a godly mom. It has nothing
to do with household chores. As I look back with the perspective I have
now, I can see how God was shaping me as he helped me shape two

precious lives. I still can't believe he trusted me so much with them. They were (and are) his kids, and he gave them to me to raise. There weren't a lot of encouragers beating the drum for motherhood out there then, so I didn't really understand the incredible honor and privilege of being responsible for two little lives.

But I soon discovered the deep sense of "job satisfaction" that came from spending time with my children. Sure, I got tired and on some days longed for time to myself. But I loved watching them when they weren't aware, seeing the absolute joy and hearing their precious laughter as they played games with their friends. Joining a tea party or a puppet show with their dolls and stuffed animals made me smile. Bedtimes were precious times; answering serious questions, explaining things about God and his universe, prayers, hugs, and "I love you's" brought indescribable contentment. I knew I was where I was supposed to be, doing a job no one else could do.

Motherhood is such a great gift. In the midst of it, we sometimes forget. I once asked my eighty-six-year-old mother about her favorite memories, thinking they would be from her childhood or romantic courtship days. She said that without a doubt, the best time of her life was when her children lived at home.

My prayer for you is that you will enjoy the great gift you have been given as a woman with children. Have fun with it and zero in on your children while they still think you hung the moon in the sky. Learn to savor every day with your kids.

As mothers, like it or not, we do set the tone for the family. It's both our privilege and our responsibility. When "Momma ain't happy," we need to deal with our unhappiness. Identify and eliminate the things that pull you down. Spend time with God and with people who are loving and supportive, people who lift your soul and spirit. Read encouraging books and magazines. Count your blessings every morning. If you find you are truly unhappy all the time, be proactive and get professional help from your physician and your pastor.

Remember, you're blessed to have the number one role in special little people's lives. What a privilege!

God's Promises

If my life is centered in God's love, I can draw on his limitless resources of joy.

She is clothed with strength and dignity;
    she can laugh at the days to come. . . .
Her children arise and call her blessed;
    her husband also, and he praises her:
"Many women do noble things,
but you surpass them all." (Proverbs 31:25,28-29)

The cheerful heart has a continual feast. (Proverbs 15:15)

A Mother's Prayer

Thank you, God, for the privilege of being a mom. Thank you for all the blessings you have put into my life. Please give me a cheerful and thankful heart and a sense of joy no matter what my circumstances. Help me encourage my family in living joyfully.

Please give my children thankful and joyful hearts that don't depend on their circumstances. Help our family always see the silver lining in the clouds, the positive side of life.

Positive Parenting Plans

- Keep a running list of things you are thankful for.
- Help your children make their own lists. Write down or draw things large and small and thank God for them. Have your children add to their lists over time.

Chapter 12

Banish Mrs. Grumpy-Pants

Love Is Not Easily Angered

Tell me, what is the power of grace for if not to change grumpy people?
Grace can overcome grumpy any day of the week. Radical change is one
of God's best things. God's power is greater than our sinful natures.
—ANGELA THOMAS GUFFEY, *TENDER MERCY*
FOR A MOTHER'S SOUL

Strength of character may be acquired at work, but beauty of character is
learned at home. There the affections are trained. . . . There the gentle life
reaches us, the true heaven life. In one word, the family circle is the supreme
conductor of Christianity.
—HENRY DRUMMOND

One of my grandkids' favorite video series is *VeggieTales*. Perhaps you've seen their *Jonah* movie? I remember particularly the scene where Jonah is sulking inside the whale and his friend calls him "Mr. Grumpy-Pants."

Some days I think my nickname should be Mrs. Grumpy-Pants. Ever have times when everything irritates you? When your kids are driving you crazy by doing or saying things that on another day wouldn't even cross your mom radar screen? Those are the days when we have to determine to be grown-ups. We have to dig deep into our character and force ourselves to grin and bear it. We need to walk very closely with God in prayer on those days. If we don't, we may wound those we love and have much to regret.

On Grumpy-Pants days, I need to put away my list of to-dos and concentrate on spiritual warfare, because Satan is at the core of the problem. He sees when we are tired or have too much that needs to be accomplished. He plays on our frustrations, prompting us to treat our little ones as if they're in the path of our perceived progress, when in reality, caring for them should be the primary objective of our day. So how can we retain our grip on our tempers when we cannot change the stresses we're facing? With God's help we can change the one thing we do have control over: our attitude.

Changing surroundings and getting out of the house helps. Sometimes during a difficult week, my daughter puts the kids to bed and leaves them in her husband's care while she goes out to the movies or meets a girlfriend for coffee at nine o'clock at night. Even though she's tired, it gives her a break from the house routine.

Here are some other creative ideas for banishing Mrs. Grumpy-Pants:

- Learn to recognize when you're low, angry, stressed out, or all three! Sometimes it coincides with your monthly hormone changes; sometimes it's a reaction to circumstances; sometimes it just happens.
- Postpone difficult jobs, if possible.
- Turn on some happy music and sit down with a cup of tea, juice, cold water, or coffee—whatever you find most refreshing or soothing. Try chocolate!
- Wear your most comfortable outfit and shoes or an outfit that makes you feel attractive.

- Put on some lipstick or something that smells good.
- Smile, take a deep breath, and read an encouraging Bible verse you've posted on the fridge.
- Think about your blessings.
- Send up some "help!" prayers to give God control of your day and your mood.
- Do something fun and low-key with your kids. Tell them you're not feeling well and need to rest while they have a quiet time with books and toys. Keep a box of new coloring or maze books, storybooks, toys, art supplies, and other quiet things hidden away for days like this. Or sit down and color with them or sculpt some Play-Doh for therapeutic creativity.
- Call a babysitter or arrange with your husband to take the kids sometime soon. Just knowing that you'll eventually have a break from responsibility helps. Or arrange to have a girlfriend who will help you out when your emotions are unraveling—and be willing to do the same for her.

On a more serious note, if you have deeper issues from your own childhood, such as abuse, see your pastor or a good Christian counselor. Life is too short to spend it in anger or so wrapped up in ourselves that we can't see the beauty and wonder of our children.

Remember, you and God are in control. You always have choices; your choice of attitude may be the most important one.

God's Promises

If I give my day and my attitude to God, he will give me peace, strength to change, and an untroubled heart.

"Do not let your hearts be troubled. Trust in God; trust also in me. . . . Peace I leave with you; my peace I give you. I do not

give to you as the world gives. Do not let your hearts be
troubled and do not be afraid." (John 14:1,27)

I have learned the secret of being content in any and every
situation, whether well fed or hungry, whether living in plenty
or in want. I can do everything through him who gives me
strength. (Philippians 4:12-13)

Be imitators of God, therefore, as dearly loved children
and live a life of love, just as Christ loved us and gave himself up for us as a fragrant offering and sacrifice to God.
(Ephesians 5:1-2)

A Mother's Prayer

*Lord, when I am stressed out, please give me your peace and strength to change my atti-
tude. Give me an untroubled heart and a joyful spirit. Please forgive me for my
unChristlike attitudes and show me creative ways to change or eliminate them.*

*Give my children a sense of peace and safety in our home. Help them know they
are loved and secure. Please make up the difference for any mistakes in my parenting.*

Positive Parenting Plans

- List some fun things you would really enjoy doing with your kids
  and set a time to do them.
- Memorize James 1:19 and bring it to mind whenever you feel
  yourself losing your grip on your temper.

Chapter 13

A Home Where Grace Lives

Love Keeps No Record of Wrongs

If you're coming to see us, come without warning. If you're coming to see the house, call ahead.

—JULIE PERKINS CANTRELL, MOPS INTERNATIONAL

God's love is not a conditional love; it is an open-hearted, generous self-giving which God offers to men. Those who would carefully limit the operation of God's love . . . have missed the point.

—J. B. PHILLIPS, *NEW TESTAMENT CHRISTIANITY*

The gift of grace can be both difficult to give and challenging to accept, unwrap, and enjoy. Have you ever been in a home where you felt uncomfortable? Where things were valued but people were not? Where the smiles were only skin deep and you needed to be on your best behavior? Perhaps you felt you were being judged—and coming up short.

That's how a lot of people feel about God in general and Christians in particular. But God's grace is the opposite of judgment. He loves and welcomes us as we are. And once we know and accept God's love, we are free to give it to others. When we lose sight of God's grace, however, we lose our perspective on what really matters. In *The Rabbi's Heartbeat*,

Brennan Manning writes, "Lacking a lively awareness of my core identity as Abba's child, it is relatively easy to become enslaved to the approval and disapproval of others."[1]

After I quit working and stayed home to raise our family, I felt a little lost. Talk about identity theft! How did I measure myself? I had no paycheck coming in, no list of important tasks that could be checked off with satisfaction. Instead, I had endless amounts of dirty stuff to clean. Some days, my self-esteem rose and fell on how clean my house and kids were. And because I'm not a type-A personality, the house was not exactly shipshape. I felt guilty sometimes, as if I was never doing enough. If I slipped out of the house with the girls to go on a hike while there were still chores to finish, I felt like a delinquent. When my husband came home and asked how my day was, I should have told him the truth—that I felt like running away. Oh, I'd take him and the kids with me, but I'd gladly leave the house behind and move into a hotel with maids and a pool!

Then something life-changing happened. God got my full attention and showed me who I really am (his beloved child) and what is expected of me (to love). That's it. So simple and beautiful, yet so scary and unbelievable. That's grace defined in our lives—to love others and to love and be loved by him. I took a deep breath. False guilt went out the window. I began to relax and enjoy life again. I learned to concentrate on other people, not on myself or on things. Am I perfect? Oh, no. Am I forgiven and loved by God? Yes. Grace isn't just for other people; it's for me too. There's plenty to share.

Here is a taste of what Angela Thomas Guffey shares about grace in her book *Tender Mercy for a Mother's Soul*:

How to Know Where Grace Lives

- All the neighborhood kids want to hang out at the house where grace lives.

- There is always enough for one more where grace lives . . . one more for dinner . . . one more to sleep over . . . one more hug . . . one more kiss.
- You can see people dancing where grace lives.
- You can hear things like "Please forgive me, I was wrong. . . . You are my treasure. . . ."
- The eyes of the children where grace lives shine with joy and anticipation. They have not been wounded by impossible expectations. They have not been distanced by rejection. They have been embraced and accepted and loved.
- The moms at the house where grace lives are just regular, everyday moms, but God lives inside them. By His power, they are becoming holy and righteous and good. They stumble but recover quickly. They make mistakes but say, "I'm sorry." They get blown by the winds of heartache and adversity, but their hearts remain tender toward God.[2]

Isn't that beautiful? In the house where grace lives, failure is not permanent. Mistakes are allowed. Perfection is not on the premises. Growth is encouraged, but love is unconditional. The mom is having fun being a mom, and the kids are having fun being kids. Love abounds. It's a place where God can smile and put his feet up.

Today I'm going to take a deep breath and put my feet up too. I'll sit and read my grandchildren a story on my lap; it will keep them out of the dust bunnies.

God's Promises

God saved me with his gracious love when I was still a sinner, and he will continue to love and perfect me.

I pray that you, being rooted and established in love, may . . . grasp how wide and long and high and deep is the love of Christ. (Ephesians 3:17-18)

"My grace is sufficient for you, for my power is made perfect in weakness." (2 Corinthians 12:9)

At one time we too were foolish, disobedient, deceived and enslaved by all kinds of passions and pleasures. We lived in malice and envy, being hated and hating one another. But when the kindness and love of God our Savior appeared, he saved us, not because of righteous things we had done, but because of his mercy . . . having been justified by his grace. (Titus 3:3-5,7)

A Mother's Prayer

Thank you, Father God, for loving me just as I am, warts and all. Please give me grace to love my family the same way. Make our home a house where grace lives.

Please give my children a deep understanding of grace, so that they will know in their hearts that they are accepted and loved by me and by you, just as they are.

Positive Parenting Plans

- Plan a goof-off day with your family. Do something you would not ordinarily do, something everyone would enjoy. Maybe it's a simple picnic on the floor or sleeping together in a tent outside.
- Read aloud *You Are Special* by Max Lucado, a great child-friendly story about God's grace and love.

Chapter 14

God's Kids

Love Keeps No Record of Wrongs

Oh, June, things are just things. Now, if you had been broken, that would be something to be concerned about.

—JUNE HUNT'S MOTHER, RUTH, ON BROKEN DRESDEN CHINA, IN *HOPE FOR THE HEART*

How can we instill in our children a desire for holiness and right living without falling into legalism, requiring them to obey out of obligation or fear of punishment rather than love? By introducing grace. But how do we teach our children about such an adult concept? How can we help them grasp the wonder of receiving free, undeserved mercy and favor from God? And if we emphasize grace as pardon from deserved punishment, how do we prevent our children from taking it as a license to do what they want and seek forgiveness later?

The key, I think, is helping our children gain a glimpse of God's character. As we teach them about his holiness, we can also talk about his being a "God of forgiveness, gracious and compassionate, slow to anger and abounding in lovingkindness" (Nehemiah 9:17, NASB). And we can, through the power of the Holy Spirit, demonstrate both an expectation of obedience and a willingness to extend grace.

I began teaching my children about grace by demonstrating it in their everyday lives. When my children misbehaved, they knew they deserved punishment, such as a time-out or having some privilege withdrawn. Yet sometimes I would sit down with them and explain that even though their behavior deserved punishment, I was not going to give it. Instead, I would give them grace because that's what God gave me. Then we would talk and pray together about forgiveness, grace, and changing our behavior. In addition, when my children had conflicts or were treated unfairly by friends, I seized that "teachable moment" to talk about practicing grace and forgiveness.

Of course, as they grew older, sometimes they would ask for grace, hoping to avoid consequences, but it was done in a joking manner. We laughed together, and they still received their consequences. Even though God forgives us and extends grace, we may still have to live with the consequences of our sinful behavior. Over time and with repeated illustrations, my children definitely began to understand both the value of holiness and the power of grace. By God's grace, they both asked Jesus into their hearts at an early age and began to grow in their understanding of how much that grace cost God and, because of that cost, how much God values them. And they've learned that because God values them so highly, he wants the very best for their lives. This is why he's given them—and all of us—rules to follow as part of his loving care and protection.

We're grown-ups, you and I. But our secret is that inside, we're still kids in some ways. I remember my grandmother, in her nineties at the time, saying that inside she was still eighteen and that looking in the mirror sometimes came as a shock. As grown-ups, we may still be afraid of the dark unknown or of snakes or wasps or spiders. We cover these fears in front of our children because we *are* the grown-ups. But some days I want to be a kid again, don't you? I would really enjoy having someone to look after me, wash my clothes, and draw a hot bubble bath for me. Someone to prepare a snack and to insist I lie down and take an afternoon rest. Someone to clear out the bad things in the dark, smush all the spiders, and make everything right in my world. Someone to rescue me. Someone to help me make the right choice when I'm really tempted to go my own way. Then I am reminded that I am still God's valued child. And I can call on him for help.

A mom named Timmie wrote these insightful thoughts on being God's child:

In looking back over the years of child rearing, I can see that one of the most significant things I've benefited from is having experienced just a taste of the unconditional love that my Father in Heaven has for me, and a small glimpse of how he must see me as His child. I have become humbled in my own heart when I consider that, though I have felt the full range of a mother's love and care and concern for all aspects of my children's development as people, it is nothing in comparison to what He feels for me.

From the beginning, my children didn't have to "do" anything to merit my love for them, yet it was always there in abundance. Their transgressions could never have caused me to cease caring for them. It grieved me to have to discipline them, and there were times that I saw them heading down a path of behavior or attitudes that would only bring them pain or suffering, knowing that I would have to lovingly teach them where their error was. Sometimes the "lesson" was harsher than others, but it was still only done out of my love for them, and my desire for them to learn well. When my children wanted to have a close relationship with me and spend time together, it filled my heart with joy. When I saw them heeding my words of counsel, it pleased me. Being *their* mom has helped me to learn better how to be *His* daughter.

God values us and showers us with undeserved love, which is called grace. While it grieves him to discipline us, he knows it's necessary for us to grow and be transformed. While there is nothing we can do to make him love us any more or any less, knowing how much he loves and values us calls us to obedience.

We are all God's kids. Let's enjoy it and live like thankful and beloved daughters of our King.

God's Promises

I am loved by God, and his love is not conditional.

> For it is by grace you have been saved, through faith—and this not from yourselves, it is the gift of God—not by works, so that no one can boast. For we are God's workmanship, created in Christ Jesus to do good works, which God prepared in advance for us to do. (Ephesians 2:8-10)

> In him and through faith in him we may approach God with freedom and confidence. (Ephesians 3:12)

> For sin shall not be your master, because you are not under law, but under grace. (Romans 6:14)

A Mother's Prayer

Dear Lord, thank you for loving me as your child and for giving me daily grace. Please help me model everyday grace to my children. Give me a joyful spirit that is light because you are quick to forgive. Lift any false guilt I may have over not being a perfect mom and please make up the difference where I fail.

Help my kids understand how much you love and value them—so much that you gave your own Son's life for them. Please give my children hearts that are attracted to holiness. Let them be quick to repent and turn from their sins and quick to receive your grace, so they will not carry the weight of guilt.

Positive Parenting Plans

- Pay particular attention today to your children's interactions with each other and their friends. Watch for opportunities to help them demonstrate grace to one another.
- Teach your kids this acronym:

    G—God loves you.

    R—Really! (or for older kids: Regardless of your actions.)

    A—And he wants you to follow him.

    C—Christ died for you.

    E—Every day live for him.

Chapter 15

Delighting in Creation

Love Rejoices

You cannot glorify God better than by a calm and joyous life.
—CHARLES SPURGEON

Sometimes when we are most weary, the best thing to do is just sit down with our kids and enjoy the wonder of them. One special surprise in spending time with our children is getting to see the world once more through innocent eyes. Everything is new. Everything is special. They can spend an hour looking at rocks and picking out special ones to give to you. When they give you a rock that looks, to your "mature" eyes, just like the rest of the rocks in the driveway, what joy it brings you to receive it as the treasure it is in your children's eyes. I have several sitting on my desk that make me smile at the memories.

Children show us how to find delight in ordinary things and remind us of the awesomeness of God's creation. They can uncover joy in the midst of chaos. They share the love of Christ by holding out a dandelion in a sticky, dirty hand. They direct us to think about the marvels of infinity while making animals out of the clouds in the sky. A child's sense of wonder helps us reflect on what a glorious Creator we put our trust in.

We can point to the Creator while we enjoy his creation as a family in the outdoors, away from the pull of the TV and the mall. Nature centers, hikes, and zoo outings provide precious opportunities to help children understand what a marvelous God made our world. We can do some diligent research and give teens a week or two away at one of the excellent outdoor Christian camps available that match any teen's gifts and interests. Better yet, we can plan some family times together that fit our teens' interests or dreams—hiking, learning to fly fish, water or snow skiing, riding mountain bikes, or surfing.

Spending time in the natural world, whether it's at the seaside, the mountains, a lake, the zoo, or a city bike path, gives families a better sense of the size and power of God. Sometimes we seem to view God as a handy, pocket-sized shopkeeper who delivers our needs when we order online. Looking at his creation will soon dispel that image.

Over the years our family made some really special memories in the outdoors. There were many prayer lessons too. One fall we had an unexpected few days off. I called and got great last-minute accommodations in Yellowstone National Park. On our first day at the edge of the Grand Tetons, we forged across a huge mountain meadow criss-crossed by a meandering stream to get up close and personal with a small group of moose. Talk about a sense of humor; God had to be laughing when he made a moose.

Eventually, we headed back toward our faraway car. My husband, who has an endearing habit of checking on me, asked if I had the car keys. After frantically looking in my pockets, I discovered they were gone. The meadow was huge, with no trees or bushes to mark the trail we had used. This was before cell phones, and we were literally in the middle of Nowhere, U.S.A. We immediately prayed, asking God to direct us to the three-inch-long car key. The task looked impossible.

I remembered tripping in a small animal hole as we hurried along the stream. But where along the stream was it? Long story short, God directed us to the hole, and my husband put his hand in it and pulled out the key. (Well, I wasn't going to put my hand in there!) We thanked God joyfully and continued to our motel, where we learned that there had been a grizzly attack the day before. Everyone had cleared out, and that's how we got the last-minute room! The kids had a list of animals we hoped to see, and God let us see them all, including a far-off grizzly and her cubs.

Has your God seemed too small lately? Do you feel hemmed in by motherhood's responsibilities? Are worries getting you down? Look in the faces of the miracle gifts of your children and be reminded: There is a holy God who created all things, and he loves you greatly. Get out of the house, outside in nature, and make time to enjoy God with your children. His face is in his creation.

▍ God's Promises

My children and I belong to the Creator God, who is joyful, good, and faithful. We can put our trust in him. The Lord who made all of creation will value and love my children and me forever.

> Shout for joy to the LORD, all the earth.
> > Worship the LORD with gladness;
> > come before him with joyful songs.
> Know that the LORD is God.
> > It is he who made us, and we are his;
> > we are his people, the sheep of his pasture. . . .
>
> For the LORD is good and his love endures forever;
> > his faithfulness continues through all generations.
> > (Psalm 100:1-3,5)

"Look at the birds of the air; they do not sow or reap or store away in barns, and yet your heavenly Father feeds them. Are you not much more valuable than they? Who of you by worrying can add a single hour to [her] life?" (Matthew 6:26-27)

Don't be dejected and sad, for the joy of the LORD is your strength! (Nehemiah 8:10, NLT)

A Mother's Prayer

Creator God, I claim your promise that we can put our trust in you, no matter what our circumstances. Thank you that you are unchanging in your love from generation to generation. Please be our family's joy and strength forever.

Please help my children see your truths through the beauty of your creation. Bind them to you with love so they will always put their trust in you.

Positive Parenting Plans

- Take an after-supper walk through the neighborhood with your children to look for signs of God's creation.
- Plan a family vacation enjoying nature—perhaps at a beach, a lake, or the woods. Even if your adventure is a year away, involve the family in looking at brochures and maps, planning, saving, and making lists for packing. Anticipation is part of the fun.

Chapter 16

Sharing Laughter, Sharing Love

Love Rejoices

Laughter is the sun that drives winter from the human face.
—VICTOR HUGO

Laughter is the closest thing to the grace of God.
—KARL BARTH

How do you picture God? Is he ever smiling? Ever telling a funny joke or (gasp) laughing out loud? Or is your God perpetually frowning at you? If he is, that may be the vision of God you are communicating to your kids. If, as parents, we spend most of our kids' childhood years focusing on discipline, teaching responsibility, instilling a strong work ethic, and investing our energy in clean laundry (all good things), we'll miss out on sharing the joy of God's love and grace. We and our children will gain so much more from these short years if we can relax and enjoy raising our families. A lifetime is made up of individual days, and each day is a gift from God. We don't know how many days we've been given together.

Some of my best memories of raising my children are the silly things we did together. We ate green eggs and ham for breakfast. We danced. We watched raccoons in the moonlight. We carried kids and pets around using empty trash cans as trucks. We put on crazy puppet shows. On washdays, we put clean underwear on our heads while folding clothes. Try staying mad at someone while white skivvies wiggle over her eyebrows!

We held unexpected "fire drills" while driving home with their friends in the car. Finding a quiet place to pull over (we lived in the country), we would yell, "Fire drill! Everybody out!" Then we'd all pile out of the car and run around it as fast as we could, singing and screaming and yelling, usually accompanied by old Beach Boys songs.

One family I know invites unsuspecting friends over for dinner. When everyone is done eating, they all fall to the floor. The last one on the floor has to clear the table and wash the dishes. They started this when their children were young, but their grown kids still love it.

I sing terribly off-key, but I loved making up silly songs with my kids. Now I do it with my grandkids. We make up songs about whatever we're doing. The songs get sillier and sillier. Knock-knock jokes and elephant jokes and other word games make us laugh too. My husband is great at tickling, drawing imaginary animals, and making funny faces. We play a wild version of "mountain croquet" in the field behind our house, and the game rules change often. In fact, we change the rules in all the family games we play.

Every family can find their own fun. As you know, each person in the family is different. Some kids like surprises, and some hate them. Some people like word jokes such as puns, and others just don't get them. But together, we can find things that are fun and silly and enjoyable for everyone.

I love the outdoors, but I'm not a natural camper. The joy of someone else doing the cooking, making my bed, and cleaning the sink makes a hotel my ideal vacation spot. But when our kids were younger, I slept in tents and a borrowed camper. Our family loved being together, cooking over campfires, hiking, and sort-of-fishing with our dog in mountain streams (there was so much splashing going on, no actual fish were ever caught). Even though it was not my natural bent, I really enjoyed it because it brought our family closer together.

The point is to not always take life seriously; it's serious enough on its own. Be creative and let your kids see you enjoying life and laughter. A young family we know had a child in an out-of-state hospital for repeated serious surgeries. While living in the Ronald McDonald House for weeks, they brought their daughter's red wagon filled with toys and took her and her sister exploring all over the hospital grounds. They purposefully looked for ways to store away special memories even during really tough times.

Being a parent gives you the excuse to be a kid again. Start some silly family traditions that everyone enjoys. Play dinosaurs in the garden. Share some old games you used to enjoy. No matter how tough life is at the moment, make some happy memories with your family. Laughter has just recently been scientifically proven to be good for our health. But our God, who made fun things such as beaches and monkeys and fireflies and belly buttons, put that in the Bible a long time ago.

God's Promises

Trusting in God and having cheerful hearts will give my family peace in our souls, as well as healthier minds and bodies.

> A cheerful heart is good medicine. (Proverbs 17:22)

> Be anxious for nothing, but in everything by prayer and supplication with thanksgiving let your requests be made known to God. And the peace of God, which surpasses all comprehension, will guard your hearts and your minds in Christ Jesus. (Philippians 4:6-7, NASB)

A Mother's Prayer

Father, thank you for the gift of laughter. Please give me joy and creativity in raising my children. Help me trust you, giving my cares and concerns to you, Lord, and leaving them there. Thank you for your peace.

Please give my children a sense of deep inner joy as they learn to trust in you. Thank you for their creative minds and unique sense of humor.

Positive Parenting Plans

- Look at your schedule and make room for fun in your life. Mark it on the calendar: "Bowling for candy. Friday night. Be there or be square."
- Have a family game night. Try mixing two games together and see what kind of laughter develops.

Chapter 17

Holy God, Transform Me

Love Rejoices

Your goal as a Christian is to be Christ-like. This can only happen through divine transformation, and that's exactly what God had in mind from the beginning of time.

—JOYCE MEYER, *ENDING YOUR DAY RIGHT*

Have you noticed that when we focus on ourselves or on the stresses of our daily lives, we become empty, drained of energy and hope? But when we focus on God, we are full and overflowing with all that we need to embrace life and overcome its challenges. As I walk with God, praying, reading, and studying the Bible, God's Word transforms me. I become a different person, a better person, a better mother. I don't know how the Holy Spirit works; I just testify to you that when I yield myself to him, I see changes—miraculous changes—in my life.

God does much work in transforming our lives from the lessons we learn through our children. Even as we are teaching them about God, he is teaching us things about himself through them. For example, when I consider my love for my children, I get a small glimpse of how God loves me as his child. As many times as I have read the Bible, when I read it to my children—and now to my grandchildren—and talk about its truths, I still learn new things about God, life, and myself. It's like opening a bottomless treasure chest and sharing it with our children.

Stormie Omartian, one of my favorite Christian authors, lists "Ten Good Reasons to Read God's Word" in her book *The Power of a Praying Woman*:

1. To know where you are going.
2. To have wisdom.
3. To find success.
4. To live in purity.
5. To obey God.
6. To have joy.
7. To grow in faith.
8. To find deliverance.
9. To have peace.
10. To distinguish good from evil.[3]

God promises us all these good things if we just spend time with him and his Word. And if we can instill in our children a love for God's Word, they too will experience these blessings. We can pass on God's truth to our children by reading Bible stories to them and, when they're old enough, giving them Bibles of their own. We can reinforce the importance of God's Word by letting our kids see us reading the Bible. We can memorize Scripture together. We can teach them how to distinguish good from evil. As we pray with and for them daily and talk with them about God's answers to prayer, we can help them take what the Bible says and apply it to their daily lives. As they get older, we can teach them how to turn to it for wisdom when they have problems.

Let's not be afraid to help our children dream big dreams of faith, to be a little wild and crazy. Throughout the Bible God tells the stories of his walk with his people. Look at all the risks women in the Bible embraced—and the lives that were changed—because they took God at his word. One young mother defied the great Pharaoh and hid baby Moses. Ruth left her culture to help Naomi and found a new husband and a new faith. Rahab saved the lives of spies, who then saved her family and friends from death. Esther took the chance of being killed by the king to save her people from a massacre. Young Mary said yes to God and suffered the humility of being an unwed mother and giving birth to her baby in a stable far from home. In faith she embraced the pain and privilege of giving birth to the Savior of the world.

As our children watch us taking our steps of faith and trusting God, they will learn that he is trustworthy. They will also gain courage to stand up for their beliefs. Motherhood is such a delicate dance of holding on and letting go. If we always let our kids take the easy or safe way out of their problems, they will miss walking with God through dark tunnels and coming out stronger on the other side. Allowing ourselves and our children to be transformed by God is not easy. He may take us places we don't initially want to go to stretch our faith and mold our character. But it's worth it because we become more like Jesus.

As mothers, we face complex problems in raising our children in a culture that is increasingly hostile to Christian values and beliefs. But if we focus on our fears, we will spend our lives holding a half-empty cup. We must learn to put our trust in God for everything, including our kids. We must fight against the temptation to retreat into our homes rather than reach out to a hurting world and show our kids that they can make a difference. As God transforms us through that wonderful Book and our walk of faith, it will show in the way we mother our children. We will have a joyful and courageous spirit because we know that he is trustworthy.

God's Promises

As I walk on this dark earth, God will light my path and show me the best way. He will keep changing me to reflect his goodness.

And we, who with unveiled faces all reflect the Lord's glory, are being transformed into his likeness with ever-increasing glory, which comes from the Lord, who is the Spirit. (2 Corinthians 3:18)

Whoever gives heed to instruction prospers,
    and blessed is [she] who trusts in the LORD. (Proverbs 16:20)

Your word is a lamp to my feet
    and a light for my path. (Psalm 119:105)

A Mother's Prayer

Holy God, please keep transforming me into the loving likeness of your Son, Jesus Christ, through the power of your Holy Spirit. Give me time for prayer and reading the Bible. Give me all I need each day to be a joyful, wise, courageous, and loving mother.

I pray that my children will love and trust you for direction in their lives. I pray that they will be single-minded, not conformed to this world but brave because they are being daily transformed by you into the best they can be. I ask that, like young David, they would have spirits of courage, not of fear, so they can stand up and stand out for you. Please enfold them and guard them with your might and power.

Positive Parenting Plans

- Start memorizing Scripture. Do it in a way that fits your children's personalities because everyone learns differently. There are lots of resources on the Internet and at the Christian bookstore that can help you. Keep it fun for everyone and have periodic rewards.
- Make space in your schedule for some family Bible time. Consider starting a tradition of reading a verse or short devotional at the start or close of a meal and then discussing together what it means.

Chapter 18

I Wanna Be a Honey-Badger Mom!

Love Always Protects

Many Christians . . . strive to do their best to fight against sin and serve God, but they have no strength. They have never really grasped the secret that the Lord Jesus will continue His work in them every day, but only on one condition: every soul must give Him time each day to impart His love and His grace. Time alone with the Lord Jesus each day is the indispensable condition of growth and power.

—ANDREW MURRAY, *GOD'S BEST SECRETS*

Consider the honey badger of Africa. Weighing only fifteen pounds, this protective little mother is relentless, fierce, and single-minded in the care of her offspring. She battles stinging insects for honey. She can range over fifty miles—without an SUV!—to scavenge food, hunting and killing vipers, puff adders, and scorpions to feed her hungry babies. Now that's dedication! To keep her babies safe, she may make a new home every five days, carrying them with her teeth. The 2002 *Guinness Book of Records* lists the honey badger as the "most fearless animal in the world." (See www.honeybadger.com. Who knew they had their own website?)

Let's be "honey-badger prayer moms" and protect our kids with prayer. Not perfect mothers, but praying mothers. Let our first response to difficult circumstances be to pray. We can pray ahead of time for things we know will be difficult for our children. We can study them and pray for them individually, knowing their strengths and weaknesses. Our daily prayers can include requests for God's protection, for their character development, and for their friends, who potentially wield such powerful influence in their lives. Let's become relentless and fierce in seeking God's power to protect our children from the ever-present influences of our insidious, materialistic, and self-worshipping culture.

When my family was younger, I sometimes shared what I was praying with my children and asked for their prayer requests. My daughters had a love/hate relationship with one of my regular prayer requests. I prayed that whenever they did something wrong they would get caught, that their sins would be brought to light so they could learn wisdom and understand God's grace.

Now, my girls loved God, and they were good kids—but they were not perfect. And I know they got away with some things while growing up. Yet God certainly answered that prayer because they were found doing things they shouldn't—occasionally in some spectacular and very funny ways, such as being caught by the principal and the superintendent of schools while hanging halfway out of a classroom window with the pastor's daughter. When they were older, they said there were a lot of things they thought about but never did because they knew God answered that prayer. I wish my own mom had known about that prayer; it would have saved me a lot of pain in learning wisdom the hard way. But I'm so glad God is faithful to love and correct our children and us.

In so many ways God has protected my children and blessed them through answered prayers. He's proven himself faithful, and he'll do the same for you. Remember that God honors persistence, so don't give up, even when your children seem determined to pursue the wrong path or when circumstances look hopeless. Like the fifteen-pound badger who fights lions and jackals to protect her young, mothers confront the forces of darkness with a powerful weapon. We don't have to carry our children in our teeth like the honey badger, but, like her, we can be absolutely relentless and single-minded in protecting our children through prayer.

God's Promises

I can be a confident, watchful, and relentless prayer warrior for my family, protected by God's armor and strong in his mighty power.

> And pray in the Spirit on all occasions with all kinds of prayers and requests. With this in mind, be alert and always keep on praying for all the saints. (Ephesians 6:18)

> Finally, be strong in the Lord and in his mighty power. Put on the full armor of God so that you can take your stand against the devil's schemes. (Ephesians 6:10-11)

> Devote yourselves to prayer, being watchful and thankful. (Colossians 4:2)

> This is the confidence we have in approaching God: that if we ask anything according to his will, he hears us. (1 John 5:14)

A Mother's Prayer

Dear Lord, please give me wisdom and discernment to know how to pray for my family. Fill me with strength and determination to be faithful in prayer for them even when I am tired. Give me a godly spirit, fierce and strong in love and righteousness. Thank you that you listen to and answer our prayers.

Thank you for my children and the gifts you have given them. Please help them become mighty prayer warriors who make a difference for you in this world. Please cover them with your armor so they can stand strong against evil. Bring all their sins to light so they can repent, grow in wisdom, and learn of your grace.

Positive Parenting Plans

- Do a fun, short study with your kids on the armor of God. Get a picture of a knight and explain how all the armor works together. Make some swords of the Spirit to play with and hang on their walls.
- Set aside a block of time to pray intentionally and specifically for any challenges—physical, spiritual, or practical—your children face this week.

Chapter 19

Baby Steps First

Love Always Protects

The only thing we have to fear is fear itself.
—PRESIDENT FRANKLIN D. ROOSEVELT

I will model the process of cooperating with God, not hiding all my struggles but rather allowing [my children] to watch because I know there are lessons in my failures as well as in my successes.
—ELISA MORGAN, *NAKED FRUIT*

Ever watch a baby taking her first steps? There is such a precious look on her face, a strange combination of fear and excitement. Fear because this is someplace she has never gone before and excitement because of the wonderful possibilities of the whole undertaking. After her first few steps, there is often a gurgling crow of conviction: *Yes, I did it, and I can do it again even better!* Witnessing such small victories always brings a smile of love and pride to our faces.

Imagine God watching with similar pride as we take our first steps of faith. He is pleased, and we are happily pleased with ourselves and the outcome of venturing forth. Soon we are taking more timid steps, all the while still holding on to familiar objects beside us. Then one day we are running with the wind. And sometimes we fall and get hurt. Or we mess up and slip into sin. But God hears our cry, picks us up, and sets us back on the road, saying, "Learn and grow from that."

Mothers endure a constant back-and-forth contest between our fears and our desires for our children and ourselves. We want our kids to try new things and meet new people, to test themselves in the world and become the best they can be. We want that for ourselves also. But that little voice of fear is always whispering, "What if you fail? What if they get hurt? What if it's too hard for them? If you love them, you'll protect them. You'd better keep them here where it's safe."

But maybe we need to rethink just what it is we're protecting our children from. Is it possible that by keeping them "safe" and shielding them from certain aspects of life, we're actually causing them greater damage? Are we robbing them of the opportunity to grow strong in their faith? What does it mean that love "always protects" (1 Corinthians 13:7)?

Jesus, whose very being defines love, was always encouraging his disciples out of their comfort zone, leading them where they had to depend on God by faith. He took them into storms on the lake or out fishing in deep water when they were tired. He invited Peter to walk on top of wind-blown waves—and Peter did, until he became afraid and began to sink. Jesus sent his disciples out two at a time to preach in the towns with instructions to take no food, money, or extra clothes. Their ministry was packed with risk as they touched lepers and cast out demons from possessed people. And yet Jesus made no promises about their safety or success.

There was—and is—nothing safe about following Jesus. We are not immune from the dangers of the world, from painful or difficult experiences, from sickness, cruelty, or death. But God promises to be right there with us, guiding us through whatever dangers or trials we face. When our families step into the furnace of hard times, Jesus is in there with us, just as he was with Meshach and his friends and with Daniel in the lions' den.

When we choose to step out and risk following Christ, we also embrace the possibility of being changed, of being made stronger. Recently I received a letter from a young mom whose family went through a really tough year. In it, she testified to God's protection:

> This past year we have been richly blessed through broken-ness. Is that possible? Absolutely! We've been driven to our knees and we've seen how big God is. He's so big he's lifted our family in his hand and held us and is still holding us. God is with us and fighting for us. We have been tested but we are not crushed. God delivers his promises today just like he did many years ago. To see that up close is pure joy. God is big enough to handle everything.

As a mom, my first reaction is often to step in and protect my children from *any* hurts, disappointments, or difficulties. It's a hard, cruel world out there, and we do have a responsibility to protect our families and ourselves in common-sense ways, especially when our kids are very young. But I have learned that sometimes I can actually harm my children in my attempts to shield them, making them weak and keeping them from growing strong in wisdom and in their walk of faith in God. Our job is not to protect our children from the possibility of life's difficulties, hurts, or disappointments but to equip them by teaching them about God's faithfulness. We protect them when we help them learn to listen for God's voice and obey his will, not ours.

Baby steps are cute, but what we truly long to see is our grown children, strong and courageous, running their race fearlessly and making a difference in the world with their love and faith.

That's the way God desires to grow us up in faith; he wants us to become fearless, trusting him to either remove the obstacles in our way or run beside us as he helps us find our way through.

▌ God's Promises

My children and I can soar with confidence and joy rather than cower in fear because God has promised to strengthen us and protect our souls from evil.

"My prayer is not that you take them out of the world but that you protect them from the evil one." (John 17:15)

"Do not fear, for I am with you;
   do not be dismayed, for I am your God.
I will strengthen you and help you;
   I will uphold you with my righteous right hand."
      (Isaiah 41:10)

But let all who take refuge in you be glad;
   let them ever sing for joy.
Spread your protection over them,
   that those who love your name may rejoice in you.
      (Psalm 5:11)

But the Lord is faithful, and he will strengthen and protect you from the evil one. (2 Thessalonians 3:3)

A Mother's Prayer

Mighty and faithful God, thank you for your protection for my family and me. Thank you for stretching my faith through hardships so I can grow and not stay a baby in my walk with you. I know that every good thing comes from you. You filter all things that touch my family. Please protect my family but help them grow strong. Give us times of green pastures and still waters but walk with us always, especially in dark valleys. Hold my kids in your hands forever.

Positive Parenting Plans

- As a family, watch *Rack, Shack, and Benny* or *Esther* from the *VeggieTales* video series and talk about these biblical stories that demonstrate trusting God.
- Talk with your family about trusting God. Pray about taking the next steps of faith that God has prepared for you and your family.

Chapter 20

Love in Deep Water

Love Always Trusts

[Jesus] said to Simon, "Put out into deep water, and let down the nets for a catch." . . . When they had done so, they caught such a large number of fish that their nets began to break.

—LUKE 5:4,6

I love this story. Picture the scene with me: Simon Peter and his friends have been out all night fishing without success. They haven't caught one fish. Exhausted and discouraged, they pull their boats to shore and begin to mend their nets. A man named Jesus comes along, climbs into Peter's boat, and begins to preach. Peter probably thought, *Why not? The boat's no good for catching fish!*

When Jesus finishes teaching, he tells Peter to take the boat back to deep water and lower his nets. Peter tries to explain that they've been there all night without catching anything. But something about Jesus prompts Peter to trust him, so he obeys.

They throw their nets back into the dark water. Not long after, the strong nets begin to break from the weight of all the writhing mounds of fish they've caught. They signal to the other boat for help, but soon both boats begin to sink in the deep water from the weight of their catch.

Peter, overcome, repents of his sins. When safely back to shore, the fishermen leave their boats and follow Jesus to become "fishers of men."

Sounds kind of scary, but deep water is where the rewards are. God led Peter and his friends to trust him step by step. Exhausted, they went back out to the deep, throwing in their nets where they *knew* there were no fish. But their real step of faith was to trust Jesus to forgive their sins. After that, trusting him to save them from drowning in a sinking boat and leaving their only job to follow him looked pretty easy. Each step of faith led to the next.

I wonder what happened to all those fish? They were the prize the fishermen thought they needed, but they became absolutely unimportant after Jesus saved their lives and their souls. Their perspective changed as they learned to trust. They began to understand the true nature and love of God. The good news wasn't what Jesus could give them but who he was and how much he loved them.

The same is true for you and me. Because of who he is and how much he loves us, we can trust God to provide whatever our families need, whether spiritual or material things. God is not a "Santa in the sky," but because he loves us and knows our human hearts so well, he manifests his miracles, small and large, for our human needs. As we learn to trust him, we can focus less on our physical needs and more on our relationship with him.

When she was seven, my oldest daughter needed a new winter coat. But she didn't want just any coat. She had seen a beautiful red and white ski jacket with a fake-fur hood. It had to be *that* coat. My heart fell when I saw the price, and I explained that we could not afford it. I said that if God wanted her to have that coat, he would have to keep it on the rack and drop the price to what we could afford. She began to pray every night for the coat (and so did I). Every couple of weeks, we'd check the store. The price began to drop. Over several long weeks, it dropped a number of times. The other coats around it were bought, but that coat stayed there over a month. Finally, the price fell within our budget. When she heard we could buy it, the look on her face was so precious. It built up her faith and trust (and mine) in a practical way. She's come a long way in trusting God since then, but God met her where she was, at age seven and in need of a coat.

About that same time, we needed a house. I longed for one in the peace of the mountains, away from the noise of the city. I made a prayer list of practical things. But in my heart I nurtured an unwritten desire: to be near water, which is rare in dry Colorado. I omitted this item from my prayer list, thinking it was too much to ask of God.

Within a year, God provided a beautiful little log house, not far from work, with everything we needed. After we moved in, we were sitting on the front porch watching a steady stream of hikers going past our new home and up the dead-end road. I called out, asking where everyone was going. One hiker answered, "You live here and you've never been to the waterfall at the end of the trail? It's gorgeous and just five minutes from here." Water! God had heard and answered my unspoken desire. We enjoyed many glorious days hiking up to that waterfall with family and friends. In the winter we slid down the frozen water on cardboard boxes torn apart to use as sleds.

God also gave us something more vital that we hadn't thought to ask for: a wonderful group of neighbors and friends who didn't know Jesus loved them. Our next-door neighbors joined us in a Bible study and got to know Jesus in a personal, lifelong relationship. Turned out their parents in another state had prayed for Christian neighbors for them.

In so many ways over our lifetimes, God is teaching you and me to trust him with the big and little things of life. We walk with him past beautiful mountain waterfalls and sometimes into deep, deep waters.

He is always faithful and worthy of our trust. Our children can learn along with us to trust him with everything, from coats to boats in deep water. What are you trusting God for?

God's Promises

God guards my family and gives us refuge against evil. If we ask anything in his will, he will answer us. Nothing we have compares to knowing Christ.

> He will cover you with His pinions,
> And under His wings you may seek refuge;
> His faithfulness is a shield and bulwark.
>
> You will not be afraid of the terror by night,
> Or of the arrow that flies by day;
> Of the pestilence that stalks in darkness,
> Or of the destruction that lays waste at noon.
>   (Psalm 91:46, NASB)

> "Ask and it will be given to you; seek and you will find; knock and the door will be opened to you." (Matthew 7:7)

> I consider everything a loss compared to the surpassing greatness of knowing Christ Jesus my Lord, for whose sake I have lost all things. (Philippians 3:8)

A Mother's Prayer

Dear Father, thank you for hearing my prayers for my family and myself. Thank you for being our refuge.

Please continue to grow my children to spiritual maturity. Give them deep convic-

tion and faith in you. Help them remember that they can always go to you to seek whatever they need instead of looking for it in the world. Please give them friendships with other believers so they can strengthen each other and stand together.

Positive Parenting Plans

- Pray with your children and teach them to "pray continually" (1 Thessalonians 5:17). Pray with them for ball games and tests—whatever their needs are. Ask them if they would like to pray and let them use their own heartfelt words. Make prayer a natural response—nothing fancy so they're not embarrassed to give thanks when their friends come over for dinner. Keep a record of prayers and answers to prayers for the family to look back on.
- Let your kids see you praying; share with them God's answers and the things you're learning about him.

Chapter 21

Good Shepherd, Refresh My Soul

Love Always Trusts

The constant presence of God is the most practical part of your life.
—Henry Blackaby and Claude King,
    Experiencing God

The extremely dry climate of Colorado is ruthless. Our bodies need lots of extra water and lotion. Though I try to remember to slather on body oil, I sometimes forget, and my skin suffers, especially my feet. By mid-summer my heels get so cracked from the dry air that it actually becomes painful to walk. Tiny dry lines grow deeper, like fissures in the earth. They crack and begin to bleed. Then I pay attention. I exfoliate. I slather on the cream and lotion. I lavish care on my feet, and once again they come back to health.

Our souls are like that. We have dry periods in life when we need the cool water the Holy Spirit offers. Bad things can enter the small cracks and fissures in our souls to infect our whole being and cripple our walk with God. Jesus says that once we drink from him, streams of living water will flow from us. In contrast, without that continual source of spiritual renewal, our souls become parched and dry. We get stressed, our tempers flare, we struggle with chronic weariness, or we find ourselves worn by worry about things that usually wouldn't bother us.

As mothers, so often we nurture everyone else but neglect ourselves. TV and magazine ads remind us to take care of ourselves physically, and that is important. But care of our souls is even more crucial. We need to slow down and let God's love permeate our lives like a salve. We can walk alongside God instead of running ahead on our own. Just as a trusting child confidently places his hand in his father's or mother's hand, we can find comfort in holding on to God's mighty right hand.

There are many ways to allow God's love to permeate us: turning to him in prayer throughout the day; spending time in his Word; seeking faithful prayer partners and praying for each other; reading Christian books and magazines; attending church; enjoying fellowship with other women on day or weekend retreats; and listening to encouraging Christian radio as we work through our day. As you soak in God's love in the ways that best fit your circumstances and personality, you'll find that the more you seek God, the closer you'll become to him and the more you'll trust him.

My young grandson loves to ask questions until he is satisfied with the answer. One day he asked, in rapid succession, "Where is Jesus? Where is God? Where is heaven? Can I see Jesus?" After stumbling through several answers, I said, "Jesus will come back some wonderful day and walk with us to heaven." Then he looked up at me and asked in a trusting, expectant, and wistful voice, "Will he hold my hand?" I envisioned the most beautiful picture of my grandchild walking with his small hand in the warm, callused hand of the Carpenter. I whispered, "Yes, honey. Yes, he will."

Even though we are grown-ups, we are still Christ's beloved children. We can put our hands trustingly in his and walk together through parenthood, surrendering to him our worries, weaknesses, and weariness. Our joy in life comes from living our lives integrated with Christ, walking by the power of his Spirit within us. As we soak in his life-giving presence, we will find not only comfort but also soul-satisfying refreshment so we can once more embrace the challenges and wonderful opportunities of motherhood.

God's Promises

If I spend time with Christ, my soul will be refreshed and full of living water that I can share with the thirsty.

> Above all else, guard your heart,
>   for it is the wellspring of life. (Proverbs 4:23)

> [The Lord] guards the course of the just
>   and protects the way of his faithful ones. (Proverbs 2:8)

> "If anyone is thirsty, let him come to me and drink. Whoever believes in me . . . streams of living water will flow from within him." (John 7:37-38)

A Mother's Prayer

Thank you for refreshing my soul with never-ending living water. Please keep me connected to the Source so I can pour out my life for others without becoming dry. Show me when my spirit is parched and lead me to find refreshment in your presence.

Good Shepherd, please give my children a deep trust in you so they will never need to hunt for anything else to satisfy their thirst. Let them learn to walk with their hands tucked safely in yours as they find peace in the joy of your presence.

Positive Parenting Plans

- Do a short study with your kids on the different ways water is described in the Bible. Draw pictures together about what you observe: a deer panting for water (see Psalm 42:1), streams of water in the desert (see Isaiah 32:2), a tree by a stream (see Psalm 1:3). John 4:14 says that whoever drinks the water Jesus gives will never be thirsty. Jesus was talking about eternal life. Talk together about how it feels to get a nice cool drink after being really thirsty. That's what it feels like to enjoy God's spiritual water. It gives us life.

- Put your children in charge of a small, inexpensive indoor plant and experiment together with water and light. Discuss how, just as plants need water and sunshine to thrive, we need God in our lives to grow spiritually healthy.

Chapter 22

Lighten Up!

Love Always Trusts

When we have a heart for God, whatever thwarts us can become what teaches us to know and love God. Our struggles refine us.

—JAN JOHNSON, *LIVING A PURPOSE-FULL LIFE*

Sometimes as a young mom, I felt as though I had the whole world on my shoulders. And it was starting to slip.

When my first daughter was two years old, we moved away from Ohio, where we had a strong support group of family and friends, to Colorado, where I knew no one. My husband had bought a house before I arrived. The fairly new neighborhood seemed like a great place for our young family. Unfortunately, I found out that I was the only stay-at-home mother on the entire block. Everyone else was either childless or worked and put their children in care elsewhere. My husband was very busy with his new job, and we had only one car, so I was home a lot, alone with my active toddler and coping with pregnancy.

At first, I busied myself with unpacking and making a home out of the chaos. Then I looked for parks or nearby places to take my daughter to play. There were none within walking distance. I killed a black widow spider in our backyard, which made the outdoor play options seem even more unfriendly. I was still struggling with the transition when our second daughter was born, so small and so beautiful. Then she developed colic and cried inconsolably for three months. There weren't any Christian groups for young moms in our area at that time. And we hadn't found a church home yet.

Tired and lonesome, I felt like a failure as a mother. And worse, I harbored false guilt. The days were so hard, but I would scold myself and think, *Oh, tough it out. Get over it. No one is really suffering here, compared to the really difficult struggles people all over the world are facing.* But for me, at that point in my life, it was a deeply hurtful and lonely time. God doesn't measure and compare our hurts; he just holds us tenderly as he uses them to shape and strengthen us.

I kept giving it all to God: my loneliness, my frustration with being unable to calm my daughter's colicky distress, and my attempts to pacify my unhappy older daughter who had a new sister, new room, new house, and new life. There was a distinct need for joy to return to our lives. My prayer life was looking like an all-night 911 line.

One day my husband and I sat down and talked about how to make things better. What were the things we needed to feel at home and to make our daughters feel at home? What were our bottom-line priorities and needs? We needed to focus our energy and efforts on what mattered most. We needed a neighborhood where people were involved with each other. Could that be done where we lived now? Realistically, no. The only open doors were the garage doors that admitted cars at night. We needed to be involved in a place where people valued real community. We wanted to be able to share God's love with others. Although God sometimes asks us to tough it out right where we are, this time he wasn't telling us to stay.

After much prayer and thought, we did some wild and crazy things. We sold our home to a nice working couple with no children and moved into an apartment complex with a pool while I house-hunted for several months. Then we moved to a log house in a small, nearby mountain town in a neighborhood packed with young families. As I mentioned in an earlier chapter, God exceeded our dreams and desires when he led us to this home. The area offered plenty of natural areas to explore (a whole mountain range). We discovered a co-op preschool run by a group of friendly neighborhood moms who pitched in two mornings a week. I began to feel part of a network of friends again. And we had opportunities to share Jesus with our neighbors.

Over the years, through this experience and many others, I've learned to be patient yet persistent in prayer. I understand the freedom of giving my concerns to God and leaving them there. I know he loves my kids and me. I try hard to listen and put into action the things God puts on my heart. And I can move out into the unknown with confidence because I know God goes before me.

Whatever your circumstances, I encourage you to lighten up by giving your burdens to God. You can turn to him in prayer, knowing that every good and perfect gift comes from him and that he is able to do "immeasurably more than all we ask or imagine" (Ephesians 3:20). God cares about your daily struggles. Trust him, and he will direct you in the best way to go.

God's Promises

I do not have to carry any burden alone. God will help me and give me rest. He will guard whatever I trust him with day by day.

"Come to me, all you who are weary and burdened, and I will give you rest. . . . For my yoke is easy and my burden is light." (Matthew 11:28,30)

For God did not give us a spirit of timidity, but a spirit of power, of love and of self-discipline. . . . I am not ashamed, because I know whom I have believed, and am convinced that he is able to guard what I have entrusted to him for that day. (2 Timothy 1:7,12)

Let the peace of Christ rule in your hearts. . . . And be thankful. (Colossians 3:15)

A Mother's Prayer

God, I ask you for freedom from worry as I place my family in your mighty hands. Please give me a spirit of power, love, and self-discipline from the Holy Spirit when I face difficulties. Thank you for your peace for my soul and for hearing my prayers for help.

Please teach my children to trust in you and to feel secure when they give concerns to you in prayer. Please give them spirits of power, love, and self-discipline when they face adversity.

Positive Parenting Plans

- When you find yourself worrying about something, commit it to God in prayer. Write down the date and the commitment in your journal. Thank God for the way he is going to answer.
- When worries sneak their way back into your mind, do something as a family for someone in need. "Borrow" another mom's children and take the whole gang to the park while she takes a break. Bake some cookies for a family burdened by illness. Take some flowers to a nursing home. You'll be amazed at how God uses the experience to transform your perspective.

Chapter 23

Always Expect the Best

Love Always Hopes

Life is what we make it; always has been, always will be.
—Grandma Moses (artist Anna Robertson)

The American College Dictionary defines *hope* as a noun as "expectation of something desired, and confidence in a future event." As a verb, it is "to look forward to with desire and confidence." This is how we want to wake up every morning, with confidence in God and hope for the best in the day. But because we're human, it doesn't always happen that way.

There are certain days when we don't know whether to laugh or cry. Some kind of bug seems to be in the air, and the kids go nuts. Anything that can go wrong does, usually early in the day. Life doesn't stop to give us a breather just because we're mothers. It keeps bulldozing right on through, sometimes dragging us along. Little things submarine us without warning. The dog gets sick, the dryer breaks down, the van won't start, the teacher sends home a note about behavioral problems, or the babysitter cancels. Or more serious things weigh us down. We have to move. A loved one is sick or dying. Finances take a surprise hit.

So how do we handle life in the trenches?

Sometimes we just lose it. We become impatient with our kids, their teachers, our husband, and the dry cleaner. Then we feel guilty for not being on top of it all and failing to exercise self-control. We have to go around apologizing to everyone. Or we find ourselves overwhelmed by discouragement.

There is hope, as Janet Congo expresses in her book *Free to Be God's Woman*: "Positive Christian women move out even when their knees are shaking. Why? Because they have been kneeling on those knees. . . . Not only do they know who they are, they know *whose* they are."[4] We "move out" because we have hope, because we know almighty God loves us. We keep doing our jobs as mothers even during difficult times.

We need to tuck away, like an emergency kit in a nearby closet, a deep reserve of hope—of God's peace, love, and joy—for spiritual emergencies. In the Bible, we see how the apostle Paul relied on a reserve of hope when he was beaten and in prison. He had spent much time reading Scripture, praying with God, and discussing life with other believers. He knew the character and love of God, so he could trust him. He knew that whatever was happening would pass eventually. He knew that God walked with him wherever he was and would eventually bring him home. An eternal fire of hope burned within him. He had built up a reserve of trust through prayer and an experience of God's faithfulness in the past.

What can we learn from Paul about hope in the middle of life's stresses?

- Rejoice in the Lord, who loves you and your family (see Philippians 4:4).
- Don't worry about anything, but give it to God in prayer. Let go (see Philippians 4:6).
- Concentrate on what is beautiful, admirable, and excellent in life. Count your blessings (see Philippians 4:8).
- Acknowledge that God is responsible and in charge of every situation. Trust him with confidence (see Romans 15:13).

- Ask for and rely on the grace of the Lord Jesus Christ (see
  2 Corinthians 12:9).

Our children need to feel safe and secure in their world, a need magnified even more by the events of September 11, 2001. The way we respond to life's stresses makes a difference in the lives of our children, who are always watching and learning from us. Because we want them to learn how to do things God's way, let's be sure they see us rejoicing and hoping in the future even in the middle of trouble. Let's invite them to join in giving every concern to God in prayer and teach them to count their blessings. And let's remind them that God created this world and is still in control, so they can trust him and ask him for grace to get through any situation.

God's Promises

God is my refuge, strength, and protection. Nothing is impossible with him.

> God is our refuge and strength,
>   an ever-present help in trouble. (Psalm 46:1)

> He who fears the LORD has a secure fortress,
>   and for his children it will be a refuge. (Proverbs 14:26)

> "All things are possible with God." (Mark 10:27)

A Mother's Prayer

My hope and trust is in your loving character, Lord. I rejoice that you love my family and me. Thank you for being in charge of every situation we find ourselves in. Please give me a deep reserve of hope and grace to use as a refuge from trouble and worry. Thank you for every blessing. Thank you for your holiness.

Please cover my family with the love of Jesus Christ and the power of his blood that he gave for mankind. Fill my children's hearts with an unshakeable trust in you and give them a joyful sense of expectation about the future.

Positive Parenting Plans

- Read books with your kids about Christian heroes they can look up to. Point out how faith and trust in God changed the heroes' lives from ordinary to extraordinary.
- Talk with your children about the dreams they have for their future and how they can make a positive difference in the world.
- Memorize Mark 10:27 together as a family.

Chapter 24

Good Job, Mom!

Love Always Hopes

From my mother I learned the value of prayer, how to have dreams and believe I could make them come true.

—PRESIDENT RONALD REAGAN

My mom always encouraged me. I lived a hard life. She prayed for my salvation for thirty-six years before it happened.

—ANONYMOUS

Humanly speaking, I owe my salvation to the fact that my mother lived Christianity before me all of my young life.

—PASTOR JERRY FALWELL

My daughter was really happy today because we had an early, heavy October snow. It meant that school was closed. You'd expect any young student to be happy about an extra day of freedom, but my thirty-one-year-old daughter was happy because it meant that she got an unexpected opportunity to spend time with her four-year-old son. When his school closes, she works from home, connecting with the office by computer and telephone. Today she compressed her workday to make time to shovel snow and ride a sled with him. My grandson prayed for snow—lots of it—last night, so he thinks God did this all for him. And, who knows, maybe that's partially true; the snow *is* deeper in our part of town.

My daughter's joy in having time with her child—and his delight in being with her—makes it obvious that she's a good mom. But she doesn't always see herself that way. Just last night she told me she was a terrible mom. Some disciplinary thing had come up with her son, and she felt she had failed. Our conversation brought back memories of my feeling the same when she was a child, of being certain that I was a rotten mother.

When my children were young, I was always berating myself for not being a better mom. Does that sound familiar? Do you sometimes find yourself battling regret over how you've handled a situation? It's okay, of course, to want to be better. The desire to grow and improve leads us to seek advice from God and from books, parenting classes, and more experienced mentoring moms. But let's beware of the negative talk we let run through our heads. Constant self-criticism can leave us feeling defeated rather than motivated. We need to give ourselves a break and reflect on the joy of Christ within us and the love of God that covers us. When we do this difficult job well, it's definitely okay to pat ourselves on the back and say, "I'm a good mom." Especially if there's no one else around to say it for you.

My friend Kathy recently shared that as her children headed out the door for school or other activities, she regularly asked them, "Honey, remember: Whose child are you?" The expected answer was, "I'm God's child." As Christian moms we can ask ourselves that same question: "Whose child are you?" And the answer is the same: "I'm God's child."

Our heavenly Father is pleased with our desire to please him. He walks with us every day as we learn the art of mothering. It's a job learned while doing, and on-the-job training can be tough. But God doesn't expect us to be instant experts at something we've never done before. And he promises to make up the difference. In Jeremiah 29:11 God says, "For I know the plans I have for you . . . plans to prosper you and not to harm you, plans to give you hope and a future." We can claim that promise for our children and for ourselves.

He also says that he knows how to give our children good gifts, much better ones than we as human parents can give (see Matthew 7:11). God has given us everything we need to succeed as mothers. He gives each of us every spiritual blessing, but some of our possibilities are never even opened because we don't believe that God would gift and equip us so lavishly.

The truth is, God loves us just as we are, and so do our children. Maybe part of the problem with believing we are good mothers is that we tend to confuse excellence with perfection. As humans, we will never be perfect until God takes us to be with him. If we were perfect, we wouldn't need Christ. Only God is perfect. A good mom is not a perfect mom. How hard would that be for our children to live with! Our kids benefit when they see us make mistakes and ask forgiveness for those mistakes. Through our flawed examples, they learn that they don't have to be perfect to be loved.

In reading and talking with many people, I've found that the most common description of a good mother is simply a mom who loves and honors God and who loves her children and spends quality time with them. We can do that and do it well.

Good job, Mom!

God's Promises

God has equipped me with love so I can be a good mother. His strength covers my weaknesses.

Not that I have . . . already been made perfect, but I press on
to take hold of that for which Christ Jesus took hold of me.
(Philippians 3:12)

Love covers a multitude of sins. (1 Peter 4:8, NLT)

I ask that we love one another. And this is love: that we walk
in obedience to his commands. . . . His command is that you
walk in love. (2 John 1:5-6)

"Well done, good and faithful servant!" (Matthew 25:21)

A Mother's Prayer

Dear Father, thank you for loving me as your child. Please encourage me as a mom. You
promise to hear anything I ask according to your will. I desire to be a good and godly
mother. Please give me wisdom, vision, love, and patience for my children. Give us times
of great joy together as a family. I need to hear, "Well done, good and faithful servant."

Please let my children grow up to be confident in you and brave enough to follow
you. Help me give them roots of love and wings of courage to make a positive difference
in this hurting world.

Positive Parenting Plans

- Think back over the past week and take note of all the things
  you've done for your family. Don't overlook the seemingly basic
  things, such as baking cookies, packing sack lunches, playing
  board games, providing clean clothes, driving safely, speaking
  words of encouragement, and helping with homework. As you
  consider all the right things you've done, say aloud, "I'm a good
  mom. I love God, and I love my family. The rest is in his hands."
- Encourage another mom by pointing out something positive you've
  noticed about her interactions with her children. Be specific.
- At the dinner table tonight, invite each person to share something he or she appreciates about the other people in your family.

Chapter 25

Mustard-Seed Faith

Love Always Perseveres

Never, never, never, never give up.
—WINSTON CHURCHILL

[Jesus] replied, ". . . I tell you the truth, if you have faith as small as a mustard seed, you can say to this mountain, 'Move from here to there' and it will move. Nothing will be impossible for you."
—MATTHEW 17:20-21

When I was little, my family belonged to a small, traditional brick church with stained-glass windows. The pastor and choir wore robes. Kids received prizes in Sunday school for reciting Bible verses and for perfect attendance. The one I remember best was a shiny necklace from which dangled a tiny mustard seed encased in clear plastic, representing the potential power of faith. I wore it often.

Our Ohio town boasted no hills, let alone mountains. I remember wondering if I came upon a mountain whether I could make it move or not. I didn't know if I had enough faith. As I grew older, I came to understand that life offers plenty of mountains that I can practice my faith on.

As mothers, we go through hard times, facing mountains that seem immovable. We are not alone; absolutely every woman struggles with something. We may face medical crises or money problems or marital struggles. We may have a dearly loved child with emotional, physical, or learning issues. We may just feel tired out and alone. I greatly admire women who have fought so many battles bravely, especially knowing that there are many more to fight and that the outcome may be uncertain.

Whatever mountains lie in our path, we need to remember that God loves us with an all-encompassing love and will carry us through whatever challenges we face. We need to hold on to that and believe it. God has assured us,

> "Never will I leave you;
>> never will I forsake you." (Hebrews 13:5)

We as mothers often have questions about why God allows suffering and disease, especially when it affects our children. Joni Eareckson Tada, physically paralyzed but joyful, faithful, and energized, encourages us in our doubts with a personal perspective:

> When . . . you are driven to your knees, you are driven there . . . *by faith* because you have nowhere else to turn. *In faith* because you must trust the One who holds your hardships in His hand. *And through faith* because you are able to rise from your knees and go forth in hope and confidence. . . .
>
> God may not show you all the answers. . . . Ask Jesus Christ to forgive your doubts and fears. Ask Him to take away any sin that separates you from Him. Then rise in faith and move forward into your life through faith in the One who gave His life for you. In the One who works all things together for your good and His glory.

It only takes faith the size of a mustard seed to do this. But—hey—give God an inch, and He'll take a mile, encouraging and strengthening you each step of the way.[5]

When we are in trouble, we must persevere because love perseveres. We can strengthen ourselves by relying on our Christian community. Many times people want to help but don't know how, so it's important that we put aside our fears or embarrassment and let our pastor and friends know the kind of help we need. We can also search out a positive group of parents enduring a similar situation who can offer wisdom, experience, and helpful contacts with national organizations.

And even if the mountain still doesn't seem to budge, we can rise from our prayers, confident that God will show us a way to walk over, around, or through it because he loves us and our children.

God's Promises

Because he wants to mature us, God will not prevent my family from going through trials. But he will not fail us in hard times when we seek him in prayer.

Consider it pure joy . . . whenever you face trials of many kinds, because you know that the testing of your faith develops perseverance. Perseverance must finish its work so that you may be mature and complete, not lacking anything. (James 1:2-4)

Be strong and courageous, and do the work. Don't be afraid or discouraged by the size of the task, for the LORD God, my God, is with you. He will not fail you or forsake you. He will see to it that all the work . . . is finished correctly. (1 Chronicles 28:20, NLT)

A Mother's Prayer

Loving Father, thank you for your unfailing love and your commitment to use the difficulties of life to make me more like your Son. Please fill me with wisdom, joy, courage, and the strength to persevere. Lead me into relationships with other Christians so we can hold each other up in love and prayer.

I pray that you will give my children a deep and unshakable faith and an understanding that you love them. As they grow, may they gain a godly maturity that demonstrates compassion and understanding for others who are hurting.

Positive Parenting Plans

- When life seems overwhelming, grab a few moments alone to read Habakkuk 3:17-19.
- Teach your children to see the small miracles God performs, such as transforming a caterpillar into a beautiful butterfly or equipping tiny ants to carry objects several times heavier than their body weight. Talk about how God uses hard things in our lives to help us grow stronger.
- Think of one person you trust enough to share your heart with and determine to seek her out this week for a time of prayer and conversation.

Chapter 26

Overcoming Battle Fatigue

Love Always Perseveres

I don't know who coined the term "Supermom," but she didn't do the world any favors.
—ANGELA THOMAS GUFFEY, *TENDER MERCY FOR A MOTHER'S SOUL*

I realized that I had turned into a human television set, so filled with 24-hour children's programming that I felt as though I had no thoughts left of my own.
—JUDITH WARNER, *PERFECT MADNESS: MOTHERHOOD IN THE AGE OF ANXIETY*

Sick kids, high fevers, doses of yucky medicine, all-nighters sometimes accompanied by vomit. Desperate voices calling out at two in the morning for blankies, drinks, binkies, and favorite toys that are misplaced. Bad dreams that lead to little feet padding into your room at all hours of the night. The sudden realization that you were supposed to provide cookies for today's school event. The constant battle of the wills regarding homework, chores, or curfews. Occasionally throw into this wild mix the misery of that time of the month, a headache, or a cold. On these days, nothing sounds as good as crawling under the covers and hiding there for a good long time.

Starting with those every-two-hour feedings at birth, fatigue sets in and lasts until the kids are all in school. College, that is. (Just kidding!) But we moms can't quit or go on strike or take off on an extended solo vacation—or run away from home. How can we keep ourselves from being used up like the witch in *The Wizard of Oz* who shriveled up and disappeared? (Come to think of it, that sounds rather relaxing about now, doesn't it?)

How can we prevent physical, emotional, and spiritual fatigue? Let's look at physical tiredness first. We're exposed to lots of germs, but we can't really take time off from our job of mothering to be sick. So we take vitamins, eat healthy foods, exercise, and engage in preventative care, such as having regular check-ups for breast cancer. When all else fails and we get laid low by sickness, we call in reinforcements: our husband, our sister, our own mother (who will always be there for us), our friend, our moms-day-out co-op, our babysitter.

For emotional fatigue we can schedule regular times away from our kids, even if we just stay hidden in our bedroom or basement and nap or read a book while someone else watches them. We can evaluate our schedules and make sure the things on it are really priorities for our families and us; if not, we can choose to get rid of them rather than waste our limited energy.

Whatever our situation, it's crucial that we nurture ourselves so that we can nurture others. Our families need us to be healthy, happy, and spiritually whole. But we're all different, and what nurtures you depends on your personality and needs. Personally, I love regular enjoyable exercise, such as a dance class, walk, or hike. When my children were young, I found that I gained new energy by getting the kids and myself out of the house and into the woods, a park, or the country. It's fun to find a tree and climb it or sit under it. I've also found that even something as simple as replacing a sugary drink with a glass of water is refreshing—although realistically most moms need caffeine! The key is to pay attention to our bodies and attitudes and recognize the signals that indicate we need to make some adjustments.

The symptoms of spiritual fatigue may be more subtle than those of physical or emotional fatigue, but if we ignore them, we're heading for disaster. As mothers, we become so involved with our children that it's easy to forget where we are on our personal spiritual journey. If we find ourselves becoming impatient, angry, or just plain rude with our families, there may be something lacking in our spiritual diet.

Just as we need physical check-ups to stay healthy, we need regular check-ups to stay spiritually healthy. Here's a quick spiritual checklist to run through when you can't quite put your finger on what's wrong in your life:

- Have I read my Bible lately?
- Have I stayed connected with God in prayer throughout my day, or have I been acting like a lone ranger?
- Am I being honest with God about how I feel instead of stuffing things deep down inside?
- Am I keeping my accounts cleared, regularly confessing my sins to God and mending relationships with my family?
- Have I been reading morally acceptable books or magazines, or have I been filling my head with spiritual "junk food"?
- Am I sharing prayer requests with someone who holds me up to the Lord?
- Have I been attending church regularly? Am I getting involved or just warming the bench?
- Am I in a good Bible study with other moms or couples?

You may have noticed that several items on this checklist involve connecting with other people. Maintaining some adult relationships is essential to our spiritual health as mothers. Satan loves to isolate us; anyone is easier to prey on if she is alone.

One of my friends commented that when she is alone ironing or doing other boring household tasks, her body is engaged but her mind is free. She's found that Satan uses those times to promote grumbling and run negative thoughts through her head. (My first reaction was, of course, to shout, "Hooray! The perfect reason never to iron or clean!") But once she realized what was going on, she put a stop to it by voicing out loud her decision not to think that way. Instead, she uses those times to pray for herself and others, memorize Scripture, plan positive things for the future, or listen to inspirational CDs. (But my personal advice is still beware of ironing!)

Like my ironing friend, you and I need to be alert for the Enemy's attacks and be prepared with a plan of defense. You may want to make a list of emotional and spiritual pick-me-ups for yourself. Keep some positive books and magazines by your bed. When a task seems over-whelming, bite off little pieces at a time. Is a problem looming over your head? Pray for advice and then take one step toward resolving it. Share your feelings with your spouse, a relative, a friend, or someone from your church. Drop all your to-dos and take the kids somewhere fun, even if it's just the backyard.

With a job like mothering, we're bound to face difficult days and occasional exhaustion, but we can recover more quickly if we've been proactive about nurturing ourselves.

Even Jesus battled fatigue. The Bible talks about his frequent retreats to pray and be by himself. And remember when he fell asleep on a boat in the middle of a stormy lake, only to be shaken awake by panicked disciples? Fatigue is not something we need to be ashamed of or cover up. It just means we've been busy in the battle.

God's Promises

God's love for me is so big it cannot be measured. He will fight my battles and give me rest.

> "Come to me, all you who are weary and burdened, and I will give you rest." (Matthew 11:28)

> This is what the LORD says to you: "Do not be afraid or discouraged because of this vast army. For the battle is not yours, but God's." (2 Chronicles 20:15)

> I pray that you, being rooted and established in love, may have power, together with all the saints, to grasp how wide and long and high and deep is the love of Christ. (Ephesians 3:17-18)

A Mother's Prayer

Lord Jesus, please give me wisdom, rest, and help when I need it and endurance when others need me. Give me a spirit of perseverance and a heart of love to serve my children when they need extra care. I trust in you; please fight the tough battles for me.

Thank you for my children. Please protect them, ease their fears, and make them strong in body and spirit. Help them sleep each night, secure in the knowledge that they are loved. Heal their hurts and protect them from bad dreams and scary thoughts. I ask that they will know you as their Savior at an early age and grow stronger in faith as they grow older.

Positive Parenting Plans

- Figure out what activities rejuvenate you physically, emotionally, and spiritually. What fits with your personality, budget, and schedule?
- Make a renewal action plan for yourself and put it into practice.
- Make sure your husband and kids are proactive about their physical, emotional, and spiritual needs too.

Chapter 27

Finding Time Alone with God

Love Always Perseveres

When you are a mother, you are never really alone in your thoughts. You are connected to your child and to all those who touch your lives. A mother always has to think twice, once for herself and once for her child.
—SOPHIA LOREN, ACTRESS

Solitude. Okay, quit laughing. I know solitude is hard to come by, especially when you're the mother of children under five. I remember retreating to the bathroom, grateful for a moment alone, and watching, dismayed, as little fingers groped under the door, accompanied by "Mom, what are you doing? When are you coming out? Why can't we come in? Are you done with your privacy?" I loved being with my kids, but sometimes we all need a breath in private.

As challenging as it is, we must find time to be alone with God. It's impossible to know what we are thinking or to hear what needs our soul is whispering when we are amid the clamor of the world and the expectations and needs of others.

Jesus made a habit of getting alone with God even in the busiest days of his ministry. In the same way, virtually every Christian friend

I've asked has named private time with God early in the day as the *number one* help when her kids were young. I too have found that my outlook on life can be truly transformed when I start my day with prayer, Bible study, and devotional reading.

God talks to us in a still, small voice that is meant to call us away from the world and its responsibilities. We need to see the bigger picture by getting farther away from it for a short while. Though it may seem impossible, reexamining your daily schedule will likely reveal an opening where you can plan a regular quiet time in which prayer and Bible reading are the priority. Journaling is another great tool to help you collect your thoughts and connect with God. Early morning is a good time. If a child pads down the stairs to see what you're up to, have a children's picture Bible at the ready and explain that Mom needs time alone with God but that he can quietly keep you company.

Making ourselves get up a little earlier than the kids and sitting down with a cup of tea or coffee while we give the day to God is more effective than any other thing I can think of in giving us a godly spirit to walk prayerfully through our day. Praying for our children during that time is a good way to gain insight into their needs as individuals and gives us strength to face the day with an eternal perspective and godly priorities. It reminds us that we are not in motherhood alone; we walk in fellowship with the powerful God Almighty who loves us.

One of the best presents I ever gave myself was spending an entire day in prayer. I arranged for child care, phoned a friend to join me, and then loaded a bag with lunch, water, my Bible, a devotional, a journal, and a little pamphlet called *How to Spend a Day in Prayer* by Navigator Lorne Sanny.[6] Sanny suggests dividing your day into three parts: listening to God, praying for others, and praying for yourself. My friend and I found a quiet place in a park to sit and pray. We prayed separately in the morning. Then in the afternoon, we shared thoughts and needs and prayed together. In the quiet, with the day spread out before me, I had time to read the Bible and sit and listen for God's voice as I shared my heart with him.

Lorne Sanny lists five excellent reasons for planning a day of prayer:

1. Extended fellowship with God
2. A renewed perspective
3. Catching up on intercession
4. Prayerful consideration of our own lives before the Lord
5. Preparation so we will be ready for opportunity or tragedy

Time alone with God. It's one of those priceless presents we can give ourselves. It gives us light in the darkness and the ability to hear his voice in a noisy world. It blesses us with the intuitive wisdom we need to find our way as godly mothers. And it can give us the keys to unlock not only our own hearts but also the hearts of our children.

God's Promises

I do not need to be afraid or discouraged, for God is always with me and listens to my prayers.

> My soul finds rest in God alone;
> my salvation comes from him. (Psalm 62:1)

> The LORD himself goes before you and will be with you; he
> will never leave you nor forsake you. Do not be afraid; do not
> be discouraged. (Deuteronomy 31:8)

> The effective, fervent prayer of a righteous [woman] avails
> much. (James 5:16, NKJV)

A Mother's Prayer

Father, please provide time to meet with you every day. Speak with me about any issues or needs in my children's lives. Please give my children a hunger for a relationship with you, a habit of prayer and Bible reading, and hearts open to godly counsel.

Positive Parenting Plans

- Schedule a day or a morning to get away and pray. Try to do it yearly—or more often if you can.
- Teach your children how to pray for others and for themselves. Encourage their involvement in asking God's help for family needs and for people around the world.

Chapter 28

The "Perfect" Mom Doesn't Exist

Love Never Fails

Living up to ideals is like doing everyday work with your Sunday clothes on.
—ED HOWE

Striving for excellence motivates you; striving for perfection is demoralizing.
—HARRIET BRAIKER

Sometimes I've felt that I don't quite fit in. My thinking may seem a little off compared to how others view things. I bang up against rules and regulations and "that's the way we've always done it." Sometimes it feels as though I'm trying to squeeze my square peg into a round hole.

In the first grade I was the only girl to wear jeans to school. I had to sit by myself and do different work because I was ahead of the class in reading. As I grew older, I continually bugged my mother with weird questions about life and the world. She would tell me to stop thinking that way because I would drive myself crazy. (She probably meant I would drive her crazy!) When my teen years hit, I continually cycled through feeling ugly, pretty, odd, average, loved, and unloved. At times I felt guilty for having a nice home even as I envied those with nicer clothes and more money. Questions about identity, purpose, and how I compared with others left me wondering where I fit in the world.

Then the coolest thing happened: As I grew up, I figured out that *most* people felt the same way I did, at least some of the time. We all feel "different." We all sense that in some way we don't fit in or measure up to a particular standard, whether real or imaginary. Celebrity interviews often feature rich and famous people saying that they never fit in, they felt they were ugly or weird growing up, or they got ahead not because of their talent but through circumstance and luck. Underneath the layers of wealth, beauty, and fame, people still struggle with their failure to fit the perfect mold or standard.

When you get to know people well, through small Bible studies, prayer groups, or friendships, you find they too struggle with issues of perfectionism, low self-worth, isolation, or not fitting in. Then it crashes in on you: *No one* is perfect.

Yet even if you've realized that perfection is an illusion, motherhood tends to bring out all your deepest insecurities and challenge your self-esteem. There are lots of cultural and "Christian" expectations put on us as mothers, not to mention the unrealistic goals we impose on ourselves. We compare and measure ourselves against the mothers we see around us and those presented in books and parenting magazines. Not only do we feel inadequate compared to all those "supermoms," but we second-guess even the most basic decisions we make in caring for our kids. *Am I doing the right things to keep my children safe? Did I buy the right car seat? Are they healthy? Am I feeding them right? Am I a bad mother because I didn't breastfeed or can't get my kids to eat organic vegetables? Did I put them in the right school? Should I homeschool them? Is the snack I sent good enough for the class?*

We may begin to see our children as extensions of ourselves, just another way to be judged. *Are they dressed right? Are they smart, attractive, polite, and good at sports? Do they know enough about Jesus? What do my children's teachers think of me as a mother?* We even begin to look into the future and borrow things to worry about ahead of time. *Am I exposing them to enough career options? Am I praying all the right things for them? What about their future mates?* And this is all before they finish preschool!

Each of us has in the back of her mind some standard of the perfect mother (and, unfortunately, the perfect child). There is always some new "expert" ready to tell us how to become a better mom. At some point, we need to stop and say, "Enough."

So how about if you and I make a pact with each other and the Lord not to do this comparing and worrying stuff? Let's not worry about how other people see us. Let's be realistic in our demands of our children and ourselves. Let's concentrate on being godly mothers instead of perfect mothers.

There is no test we can take, like the one to obtain a driver's license, to be certified as a good mother or a good Christian, renewable every year on our birthday. Motherhood—as all of life—is a journey, where we learn as we go.

We need only look at what God says is important. We need to look to him for our approval rating as a mother. I think God's measuring stick for moms is love. Do we love God and accept his love for us? Do we love and accept our children and pass God's love on to them in our daily walk? That's pretty much it.

Sure, it's good to know about nutrition and car seats, to educate ourselves about school systems and safety measures, to pray for our children's careers and future mates. But all our kids really want now is our love and attention. They want to enjoy our company. And that's what our Father wants from us too. God doesn't do his work through perfect saints. He likes to make do with us sinners.

God's Promises

God loves me just as I am, an imperfect sinner. So great is his love that he gave his Son for me. His greatest value is love.

And now these three remain: faith, hope and love. But the greatest of these is love. (1 Corinthians 13:13)

These commandments that I give you today are to be upon your hearts. Impress them on your children. Talk about them when you sit at home and when you walk along the road, when you lie down and when you get up. (Deuteronomy 6:6-7)

But God demonstrates his own love for us in this: While we were still sinners, Christ died for us. (Romans 5:8)

A Mother's Prayer

Thank you, Father God, that your love is not based on my performance. Please open my eyes to any ways I may have unintentionally placed unrealistic expectations on my children. Please replace my worries with faith in you.

Please help my children learn that you are trustworthy and that your love is not based on their performance.

Positive Parenting Plans

- Write down your primary worries about being a godly mother. Give them, one by one, to God. Ask him to take care of each thing you wrote and to free you from worry. Ask him to show you the step he wants you to take next.
- When you put your children to bed, reassure them of your love and of God's love. Read to them, hug them, and pray with them every night. In the quiet of your bedtime routine, allow them to express any fears and insecurities and then together leave them in the hands of God. Keep this up even when your children are teenagers.

Chapter 29

Why I Love Being a Mom

Love Never Fails

*Babies are bits of stardust blown from the hand of God. Lucky the woman
who knows the pangs of birth, for she has held a star.*
—LARRY BARRETTO

Amid the pressures of the day or the frustrations of your children's particular stages of development, you may find yourself wondering why in the world you ever signed up for this. Here are some glorious random thoughts from mothers about why they love being a mom. May they help you regain your perspective and hold on to the truth that this is only a season. Some may prompt precious memories of your children's younger days, while others will touch your heart with the promise of what is yet to come. Enjoy!

- I loved singing to my kids when they were little all the songs my mom sang to me when I was little . . . and her mom sang to her when she was little . . . and her mom's mom sang to her mom when she was little.
- Because I get to be a kid again!
- I feel blessed to closely experience God's presence in the life of someone I love.
- I get a daily reminder of real childlike faith.

- To hear my daughter say, "I love to look at all that God has made when I swing."
- For the hugs I get when my three-year-old says, "I love you like dirt!" (translation: more than all the dirt on the ground; a lot!)
- The blessing of being able to affect the life of another person in such a personal way.
- Because it's just plain fun!
- Because of all God teaches me about myself (not to worry about insignificant things; to keep things in proper perspective; to conquer selfishness and pride while nurturing mercy, patience, and creativity; and lots more).
- Because of all the love you get back.
- That sense of deep satisfaction on the days you get it right.
- Because I didn't know how incomplete my life was without them.
- My kids help me rediscover God's creation just by admiring bugs, rocks, and dandelion bouquets.
- The look of pure delight on their faces when they see me.
- The joys and heartaches of being a mom bring me to a better understanding of who God is and how he loves us.
- The fun of watching them discover the universe.
- Watching *VeggieTales* videos and singing along.
- Sticky kisses with a murmured, "I love you, Mom. You're the best mom in the world."
- Those funny tickle-induced giggles.
- When my boys do something kind and generous without being prompted and I think they're actually absorbing some things we're teaching.
- Getting goofy together.
- Making up silly songs and songs about God and singing them as loud as we can.

- Because it's a privilege to be an agent for the Lord, expressing his heart in my child's life.
- I love learning things with my kids.
- Because no matter how awful I looked and felt in the middle of the night, my sweet baby was delighted to see me, and I felt so cherished!
- I love learning how to be a friend to my kids now that they are becoming parents themselves.
- Having slumber parties when their dad is on a trip.
- I love praying for my kids and having them ask me to pray for them about their needs.
- I love baby fingers poking at my face and singing the same song and playing the same game over and over and over.
- I love the peace that comes from learning that my children are a gift from God to me for a time . . . but they are his for eternity.
- I love an eternal soul looking at me through a baby's eyes.
- The delicious smell of a clean baby snuggled up on my chest for a nap.
- I love laughing with my children, reading with my children, watching their faith grow, and watching them discover that God really does know them and love them.
- I learn so much surrounded by the life of a family, instead of just living for myself.
- Because of the simple moments . . . watching them sleep, holding a cuddling baby, seeing them screech with joy and run without care, the openness when they share their feelings, watching them grow and become.
- Seeing God answer prayer in their lives.
- Because my young children let me look into their soul; they haven't learned to close their real selves off yet.

- As a mom I have just loved being there for all their celebrations and big moments: singing in preschool, when they're the dancing flowers or snowflakes in school plays; dressed up for trick-or-treat; big-eyed with anticipation at Christmas; having fun at birthday parties and slumber parties; hiking and camping out; learning to swim; singing in the choir; cheering as they play on sports teams; graduations from kindergarten, middle school, high school, or college; baptisms and claiming their own faith; falling in love; getting married; the birth of their children. I have loved laughing and crying and learning about life with them. They are separate from me but still a part of my heart walking around on this earth.

God's Promises

God has called me to motherhood and will give me strength, joy, and blessing in it.

> Those who wait on the LORD
> Shall renew their strength;
> They shall mount up with wings like eagles,
> They shall run and not be weary,
> They shall walk and not faint. (Isaiah 40:31, NKJV)

> [Jesus] called a little child and had him stand among them. And he said: "I tell you the truth, unless you change and become like little children, you will never enter the kingdom of heaven." (Matthew 18:2-3)

> Her children arise and call her blessed. (Proverbs 31:28)

A Mother's Prayer

Lord, thank you that I am your child and that you love me and find joy in being there for me.

Thank you for my children. Thank you for reminding me that they are a blessing from you. Please surround my children with family love and your love. Grow them into strong, joyful, loving, and giving people who never tire of serving you. Help them "mount up with wings like eagles" and soar.

Positive Parenting Plans

- Make acrostics of your children's names using things that are special about them. Then write down on each one why you love being a mom and save them for your kids. Put the acrostics in a place where you can be reminded on days that are difficult. Here's an example:

  N—never a dull moment

  A—always ready to laugh

  T—tenderhearted

  H—helpful and generous

  A—a hugger extraordinaire

  N—nature-lover

Chapter 30

Building a Legacy of Love

Love Never Fails

Sometimes the poorest man leaves his children the richest inheritance.
—RUTH E. RENKEL

No matter what our childhood was like, as loving Christian mothers we can choose to carefully pass down positive legacies throughout the next generations.

Some legacies take the form of wonderful memories. We build them one day at a time, one moment at a time, as we fully engage in the lives of our children. Collecting leaves, making forts, taking family trips, holding family reunions, baking the same Christmas cookies that our mothers and grandmothers made, singing our babies the songs we loved as children, serving treats on Grandma's faded blue dishes.

Having photos or mementos of those times helps ensure that the memories won't fade. Special objects that carry meaning can also serve as family legacies. We can tell stories to our children and grandchildren with things they can see and touch. My mother's small silver watch was an engagement gift from my father. It held special memories of young love for her, memories that came to hold meaning for me as well when she told me stories of their early life together while letting me wear her watch. I still prize a small, heavy iron dog, which has served as a doorstop in our family for many generations. I remember seeing it hold open my grandfather's door, and it brings back warm memories of him.

Even more meaningful than objects or memories are the spiritual legacies that pass from generation to generation. One legacy of my family was that church and the Christian faith were important. My family always went to church together. My grandparents and my great-grandparents did too. I could look up my family tree in a large and crumbling family Bible with old spidery writing in it. I handled family christening dresses and my great-great-grandfather's stone family baptismal font. Holidays revolved around the church. Family funerals were always held in churches, where we were assured that the departed were in heaven and we would see them again. I always knew there was a Creator God, even though I didn't understand all the theology involved. None of this made me a Christian, but I knew it was an important direction that must be explored. We cannot force our faith on our children, but we can guide them in the way we hope they'll walk and create a powerful legacy of family devotions and prayer.

Not all of our family legacies are positive. Think of the forms we fill out at the doctor's office with long lists of diseases and physical weaknesses that might run in our families. "Do you have a close relative who has heart disease?" "Does anyone in your family smoke?" The doctor wants to know these things because they give her clues to any family weaknesses that you and your children may inherit. As Christians, we need to become just as familiar with our spiritual health histories. Certain spiritual and emotional weaknesses and poor parenting tendencies may run in our families, and they need to be cut out before we unknowingly pass them along to our children.

We can explore our family backgrounds and ask ourselves, *What are the weaknesses that may run in my family? What are the personal weaknesses I need to guard against that have been bugging me since childhood?* We all have different areas of sin, bad habits, personality traits, and weakness that Satan likes to exploit. He studies us closely and knows us well. So we must also be students of our families and ourselves.

Some potential family-problem legacies are easy to recognize and address through preventative tactics. A history of alcoholism is a big one. Physical, emotional, or sexual abuse also stands out. These may require professional help to enable us to understand and effect change. Other negative family tendencies may be harder to spot, such as quick tempers, greed and envy, coldness of spirit, or selfishness. By facing these issues honestly now, we may help future generations avoid years of heartache and pain.

Recognizing the negative side of a mostly positive family trait is also helpful. One trait in some members of my family is reacting emotionally to things. The positive side is that I am warm and loving; the negative side is that I can react to a problem in a totally emotional and irrational way instead of thinking it through in a wise and godly manner.

Personality tests can be helpful in understanding legacies and family dynamics. My husband and I took the Myers-Briggs test after we'd been married a few years. We came out as exact opposites on every trait. Just knowing that God put us together that way helped us understand each other. We weren't deliberately trying to drive each other crazy; we just truly approached the world differently. Figuring that out strengthened our family and gave us a better understanding of our children's inherited traits and why they act the way they do.

We can't choose or change our past, but we can choose our legacies. After we acknowledge our family weaknesses, we can ask God to teach us new ways to respond to ensure that these burdens are not passed on to our kids and the generations that follow. We can discuss these tendencies with our children as they get older and help them seek God's healing.

We are the adopted daughters of God; we are his heirs. We can love our children, pray for them, and build on their strengths. We can give them strong spiritual habits they can pass on as positive godly legacies to the next generation, along with Grandma's dishes and all the treasured and joyful family memories.

God's Promises

I am God's adopted daughter. He gives me healthy, godly legacies and will help me pass them on to my children.

> Yet to all who received him, to those who believed in his name, he gave the right to become children of God—children born not of natural descent, nor of human decision or a husband's will, but born of God. (John 1:12-13)

> Since my youth, O God, you have taught me, . . .
>   do not forsake me, O God,
> till I declare your power to the next generation,
>   your might to all who are to come. (Psalm 71:17-18)

A Mother's Prayer

Lord, thank you for the new legacy you have given me as your child of grace. Help me pass the things you have taught me on to my children so they can start a little ahead of where I was. Give me your wisdom as I raise them. Help me understand their strengths and weaknesses and teach them to follow you.

I pray for my children, that you would break any hold past sins and family weaknesses would have on them. Let what has been hidden come to light. Put your wall of protection around them. Grow their strengths and give them courage to walk in your ways, even though sometimes they will have to walk a different path from their friends and acquaintances. Give them hearts that are soft toward the things that matter to you and hard toward the things of evil. Prevent any ungodly legacies from being passed on to them. Please give each child a special gift that he or she can use for your glory and pass on as a new legacy.

Positive Parenting Plans

- As you pass on family stories ("Tell us what it was like when you were little, Mommy") and look at old photos with your children, discuss strengths and weaknesses of both sides of your family. Talk about the good traits, including new ones of their own, that they might want to pass on.
- Find stories centered on families in the Bible as well as in books such as *Little House on the Prairie, Little Women, The Swiss Family Robinson,* or *The Boxcar Children*. Read them with your children and discuss the different legacies and traits of those families.

Chapter 31

Letting Go

Love Never Fails

The most important thing parents can teach their children is how to get along without them.

—FRANK CLARK

There is a critical time in the life of a young plant called hardening off. It happens when you bring a new plant home from the garden center or from a greenhouse or warm shelter where it's been raised from seed, and you place it outside in the elements for the first time. Up until that moment, the plant has been in a protected environment, but now it's subject to the realities of life—and life cannot be controlled. But if the young plant has been fed properly and given good soil in which to grow strong roots, it will be as prepared as possible for life on its own.

The same is true of our children. We prepare them to weather the realities of life by covering them with prayer. We encourage and help them build character. We spend time teaching them to rely on God through our example as well as our words. We give them responsibility. Because eventually they have to walk in this world on their own.

Being a Christian mom is a 24/7 job with challenges beyond our human capacity. It's such a relief to know that as our kids get older, although they are not holding our hand anymore, they are holding on to

God's. And he will never let them go. We can set an example by praying for help when we need it; by letting them see that when we rely on God, he comes through; and by letting them experience the reality that even when we hit a wall, we have a trustworthy Savior Lord and Father who is there to comfort and help us.

One of my frequent prayers has been that God would make up the difference. That he would pick up the pieces I missed. That he would use my mistakes and my children's mistakes for good. And he has been ever faithful.

Several pictures of my dearly loved older daughter crowd for attention in my mind. Standing by the bus with my small and trusting child as she prepared to leave for her first day of kindergarten and then waving good-bye to her childhood as the bus drove off and I walked home to cry. (I called my mom, and she shared how she cried watching me walk to school the first day.) Letting this child spend the night with a friend for the first time. Giving her the keys to the car. Waiting to hear her come home before falling asleep. Taking her picture for the first big prom. Helping her carry her belongings up three flights of stairs to her college room, feeling heaviness in every step, wanting to stuff it all back in the car and pack her home with it. Smoothing her hair as I left the dressing room before she walked down the aisle with her father to marry a young man who loved her.

Through all these moments—and then going through it again with our next child—I wondered if I had said enough, loved enough, spent enough time. Did I teach her and her sister all the things they need to know?

We never can, you know. Mothers aren't perfect, but God is perfect in his love for our children. He created them and knows how many hairs are on their heads. The Bible says he knows when even one sparrow falls, so imagine how much more attentively he will hold and protect us.

He is holding my children and grandchildren in his hand. And I can let go. When I fear for their future, I pray for them. And I pray for wisdom, peace, and comfort for my own soul as they become more independent. I give them into God's hand, and I can let go.

God's Promises

God will be with my family and me wherever we go. He is our refuge and strength, our hope and our future.

> God is our refuge and strength,
>   an ever-present help in trouble.
> Therefore we will not fear, though the earth give way
>   and the mountains fall into the heart of the sea. . . .
> "Be still, and know that I am God." (Psalm 46:1-2,10)

> "Have I not commanded you? Be strong and courageous. Do not be terrified; do not be discouraged, for the LORD your God will be with you wherever you go." (Joshua 1:9)

> "For I know the plans I have for you," declares the LORD, "plans to prosper you and not to harm you, plans to give you hope and a future." (Jeremiah 29:11)

A Mother's Prayer

Father, please help me discern my children's strengths and weaknesses. Please build them up where they are weak and help them use their strengths for good purposes. Give me wisdom to help them grow and to let them go.

I pray that your Holy Spirit will fill my children's hearts with courage to do what is right. I ask that their faith in you will grow deep and strong throughout their lives.

Positive Parenting Plans

- Look over your children's life prayer lists and write on a new sheet of paper those specific things that prompt your deepest concerns. Then give them to God and trust him.
- Start teaching your children the fruit of the Spirit (love, joy, peace, patience, kindness, goodness, faithfulness, gentleness, and self-control) and praying them for their lives.

Notes

1. Brennan Manning, *The Rabbi's Heartbeat* (Colorado Springs, CO: NavPress, 2003), 100.

2. Angela Thomas Guffey, *Tender Mercy for a Mother's Soul* (Colorado Springs, CO: Focus on the Family, 2001), 130–131.

3. Stormie Omartian, *The Power of a Praying Woman* (Eugene, OR: Harvest House, 2002), 89–90.

4. Janet Congo, *Free to Be God's Woman: Building a Solid Foundation for a Healthy Self-Image* (Ventura, CA: Gospel Light, 1985), 215.

5. Joni Eareckson Tada, *Ordinary People, Extraordinary Faith: Stories of Inspiration* (Nashville, TN: Nelson, 2001), 201–203.

6. See Scharlotte Rich, *Growing by Heart* (Colorado Springs, CO: NavPress, 2004), 193–198.

More Resources for Moms

Books

Guffey, Angela Thomas. *Tender Mercy for a Mother's Soul*. Colorado
   Springs, CO: Focus on the Family, 2001. An encouraging resource
   that offers helpful advice for moms.

Omartian, Stormie. *The Power of a Praying Parent*. Eugene, OR: Harvest
   House, 1995. Provides guidance on praying for your children.

Rich, Scharlotte. *Growing by Heart*. Colorado Springs, CO: NavPress,
   2004. This devotional for women includes Scripture memory
   cards and prayer helps.

Organizations

Moms In Touch International. This organization draws together
   mothers to pray for their children and their schools. For more
   information, visit www.momsintouch.org or call 1-800-949-
   MOMS.

MOPS (Mothers of Preschoolers) International. Through a local network of mothers and multiple resources of support and encouragement, this organization aims to nurture mothers whose
   children are preschool age or younger. For more information, visit
   www.mops.org or call 1-800-929-1287.

About the Author

Scharlotte Rich is the author of *Grandma's Gospel* and *Growing by Heart*. She lives in Colorado with Dan, her husband of forty years. Scharlotte has a master's degree from the University of Colorado but is getting her real education from her grandchildren.

REFRESHING ENCOURAGEMENT FOR A MOTHER'S HEART AND SOUL.

The Velveteen Mommy

Jenn Doucette
1-57683-649-5

The Velveteen Mommy offers mothers opportunities to find some of those rare but welcome moments to escape and recharge. You'll feel comforted by conversation, touched by some tears, and lightened by lots of laughter.

Growing by Heart

Scharlotte Rich
1-57683-683-5

Beautifully designed, this garden-themed devotional contains over one hundred pullout Scripture memory cards to teach women how to memorize Scripture.

Mothers Have Angel Wings

Carol Kent
1-57683-001-2

This special collection of stories about motherhood will inspire, encourage, and challenge you as you explore biblical truths and how they relate to being a mom.

NAVPRESS
BRINGING TRUTH TO LIFE
www.navpress.com

To order copies, visit your local Christian bookstore,
call NavPress at 1-800-366-7788, or log on to www.navpress.com.
To locate a Christian bookstore near you,
call 1-800-991-7747.